DUMONT'S LEXICON OF
PERENNIALS
Origin • Habitat • Planting • Care

Andrea Rausch

Photographs by
Annette Timmermann

© 2004 Rebo International b.v., Lisse, The Netherlands

Text: Anne Iburg
Photographs: Roland Spohn
Illustrations: Annette Timmermann and Roland Spohn (pages 115, 205, 209, 251, 269)
Typesetting: AdAm Studio, Prague, The Czech Republic
Cover design: AdAm Studio, Prague, The Czech Republic

Translation: Simona Gilarová for Agentura Abandon, Prague, The Czech Republic
Proofreading: Emily Sands, Jeffrey Rubinoff

ISBN 90 366 1690 5

Contents

Introduction

Our gardens would be unimaginable without perennials. They have so much to offer - besides plenty of flowers, they have striking leaf colors and beautiful shapes and they tempt our noses with marvelous scents. Whether wild, natural-looking perennials or cultivated, 'tame' perennials with gigantic and colorful flowers, they have much to bring to the garden. If chosen correctly, there will be plants in flower continuously and they offer charming colorful and formal combinations according to season. Besides, the perennials perform a valuable environmental function as a nutrition source for honeybees, bumblebees, butterflies and many other kinds of insects. Many plants also grow in balcony boxes or pots. The beauty of the flowers and leaves beauty can even be taken indoors - as cut flowers.

WHAT ARE PERENNIALS?

Perennials are genuine survival artists and have often adapted to extreme conditions. They frequently last for many years thanks to their subterranean storage organs - roots, rhizomes, bulbs or tubers. These tough organs sit either in the soil or near the surface of the earth. Unlike woody plants, the aboveground parts are stems and leaves and they freeze and die in winter, but this does not prevent the flower from sprouting and flowering again the next spring. A lot of perennials create ground cover and remain green even in winter.

Rhizomes appear quite often. They are thickened underground stems whose tops contain buds sprouting in spring. If the rhizome grows vertically, the plant develops like brushwood; it spreads evenly and increases in width. Bulb and tuber plants are not considered perennials from a gardening perspective, though botanically they are perennials.

ENVIRONMENT

If we know the natural habitats of our garden perennials, we can work out what they demand in the garden. Experts therefore allot them the following niches: flowerbeds, borders, open garden, under and beside trees, in rock gardens and rockeries as well as on banks and near water.

In a garden itself, there are often very small areas with different microclimates - a sunny terrace or a shady humid place under a big tree. Besides this, soil properties play a role, i.e. sandy or clay, alkaline or acid. Many perennials do well without any problems in many environments, while others tolerate only specific conditions.

■■ BEDS AND BORDERS: Almost all abundantly flowering ornamental perennials that are grown by intensive cultivation belong to this group. They prefer nourishing, rich soils where

the surface is hoed regularly. Additional manuring and watering are also important. Bed perennials do not like any rivals and therefore should not be planted in too close proximity. In a flowerbed, they can get the cultivation conditions they require for optimal development (best results).

■ OPEN GARDEN: This term means an open, sunny, warm area without the shadow of trees or shrubs, but not as tended and cultivated as a bed. In the open country, there are numerous variations from a dry steppe to humid banks; free places in acid soil are an environment for healthy plants. It is sufficient to dig up the earth before planting, remove weeds and integrate compost into the soil. Wild perennials often do quite well in this environment.

■ ROCK GARDENS AND ROCKERIES: Perennials – loving warmth and sensitive to dampness – also prefer stony, rocky, nutrient-poor soils in the open country. Stones offer the necessary change between warming in the day and cooling at night. In this group, we can come across numerous Alpine plants growing in the smallest stone rifts and sometimes even along walls. An Alpine plant grown in a shallow bowl can be very demanding.

■ WOODY PLANTS AND THEIR PERIPHERIES: Many perennials do well at the edge of trees and shrubs in rich soil. At the same time, some of them prefer sunny warm areas, while others also grow very well in cool, intermittent shade. Genuine forest perennials do well directly in the shade of a tree. They often display especially nice leaves and have one thing in common: enormous vitality. It is often advisable to plant them several years later than the trees and shrubs so that the trees and shrubs have a good chance to become established.

■ BANKS AND WATER: A garden pond has two more possible plant environments: "water" and "banks." There are water plants rooted in the underwater earth whose leaves and flowers are situated at the water level, while others are completely submerged. The perennials thrive in continuously flooded shallows and/or in humid swamp zone belonging to transitional zones.

PURCHASING PERENNIALS

It is best to buy perennials from a specialist - either in a store or through the mail. That way, we can assume that the plants are strong and healthy.

Perennials are usually sold in small plastic pots, but you can also buy big, flowering perennials in containers. They have, the advantage of growing quickly, but on the other hand, they are usually more expensive. Plants with bare roots (as opposed to root balls) are rather rare; bulb and tuber flowers are mostly sold in plastic bags.

Plants should already have root balls. You will recognize this because the root balls can be eased out from the pot. Ideally, the perennials should be planted immediately, but if this is not possible, you should temporarily put the pots in

calm, shady places. Do not forget to water them! Perennials delivered in a package should be unpacked immediately. If they are delivered frozen, they must first be defrosted in a cold room.

Consider beforehand where your perennials should grow. Is the chosen place situated in the sun or in the shade? Is it dry or humid? Will the plants grow under deciduous trees? What are the soil properties? If you take these factors into consideration, nothing should go wrong. Think it over and try one or two test plants first.

PLANTING PERENNIALS

■■■ PLANTING PERIOD: Perennials in pots and containers can be planted with frost-free weather all year round. Perennials flowering in summer and in fall should preferably be planted in spring. Perennials flowering in spring and summer should preferably be planted in fall. In case of heavy rains or very humid soil, you should postpone the planting period. If the planting period is followed by a frost, you should cover the plants, e.g. with pine branches or with fleece.

Perennials sensitive to cold, like many ferns and grasses, withstand planting in spring better. In heavy, loamy soil that gets warm slowly, they should not be planted too early in spring and not too late in fall.

Plants with bare roots without balls are best planted after the flowering period, which, in the case of perennials flowering in early spring, means late spring or early summer. In the case of perennials flowering in summer and fall, it means fall or early spring.

■ SOIL PREPARATION: Remember that a perennial must do well in a chosen place for many years. Therefore, it is important to prepare the soil well. There are several requirements for the soil: it should be aerated, water should be allowed to drain well, and should be sufficiently loose that the plants can root deeply. It should also contain sufficient humus and nutrients. This means that the soil should be dug over approximately 10 inches deep and all weeds must be removed. At the same time, compost, rotted manure or fertilizers should be added.

Root weeds such as thistle and dandelions must be removed completely with their roots; weeds creating offshoots, such as couch grass, must be eliminated at the beginning or they will grow in the perennial clump and it will be difficult to remove them later. New plants can develop even from the tiniest fragments. If the soil is very weedy or compressed, the best solution is sometimes to change it.

Heavy, loamy soil often dams up water, which perennials do not like at all. It can be loosened by adding sand, compost or farmyard manure. Additionally, the structure of a lighter sandy soil is improved by adding compost.

■ PLANTING: Before being put in a planting hole, the perennials must be watered thoroughly. The roots should not be exposed to the sun for any length of time or they will wither very quickly. It is best to plant perennials in cloudy conditions. Remember that the plants grow as deeply in a bed as in a pot.

Lay out the perennials, if possible, at the chosen place before planting. You are then able to change the position of individual plants. It is important to respect the spatial demands of the perennials and avoid planting them too tightly. Tall perennials should be planted first, followed by shorter perennials. Groundcover perennials are the last to be planted.

The final height of the fully-grown plant plays the most important role as far as the plant distance is concerned. Big plants with deep roots, e.g. Aaron's rod, can be planted more closely. In case of small groundcover perennials, a greater distance should be left (approimately 12 inches).

Press the plant well and water it sufficiently. The plants need much water at this point, especially on sunny days. However, do not water them too much as or they will rot.

CARING FOR PERENNIALS

▬ SOIL PROCESSING: Perennials do not like compressed soil, so it is important to hoe regularly. At the same time, seed weeds must be removed. Be careful not to damage roots, rhizomes, bulbs or tubers.

▬ MULCHING: A mulch layer keeps the soil moist and protects against weeds. If it is laid in the fall, and if it is approximately 2 inches thick, it also protects the root systems from frost. Good decomposed manure, coarse farmyard mulch, straw chaffs or coconut fiber products are most suitable. However, nitrogen is taken from the soil during farmyard decomposition and must be replenished through fertilization of approximately half an ounce per square yard.

■ FERTILIZATION: If the perennial bed regularly receives compost – preferably before sprouting in spring – additional fertilization is usually not necessary. If you are growing ornamental perennials with a high need for nutrients (e.g. phlox, peonies or eastern purple coneflower), additional fertilization in several doses is recommended (nitrogen-based in spring, balanced in summer, phosphorus and potassium-based in fall) for better ripening. Long-term fertilizers that relese their nutrients step by step have proved their worth. Many rock garden perennials prefer poorer soils; they would be too luxuriant in rich soils and would lose their form.

■ WATERING: Most perennials appreciate additional watering on hot days. However, they should be watered in the morning or evening rather than at noon. It is best to water seldom, but abundantly.

■ SUPPORTS: Especially tall perennials should be supported for some time so that the wind or the weight of their own flowers does not break them. Bamboo rods, wooden or metal supports are suitable for this purpose and can be made at home or bought in a store. They must correspond to the height of the perennial and be firmly anchored in the soil. Bast that will rot later is suitable for binding.

■ WINTER PROTECTION: Perennials do not normally need any winter protection, but when warm periods are followed by a frost, buds and fresh young shoots tend to freeze, especially following a frost with an icy wind and no snow. However, the plants usually recover quickly. A cover of pine branches or a fleece can help, especially in winter after planting or in regions with a temperate climate. Alpine plants are typically protected by snow in their natural location. If there is no snow, they appreciate a brushwood cover. In any case, the protecting cover should be removed quickly as soon as the frosty period is over. Perennials that keep their foliage during the winter may easily rot under a protecting cover. Fallen fall leaves are to be removed only if they cover the perennials fully. Otherwise, they are a welcomed humus source.

■ CUTTING BACK: Many perennials flowering in late spring or in early summer, e.g. lupins, larkspur, common catnip or sage, flower for a second time if cut back near the earth after the first flowering. In this way, they are prevented from dropping seeds by themselves. Fertilization promotes new shoots.

For perennials flowering in summer or fall, the flowering period can be prolonged if the faded flowers are continuously removed; the plant is then forced to create new buds. The cutting back itself can wait until the fall or spring, according to the flowering period of the perennial. Monarde, core-opsis, moon-daisy and phlox are examples.

Richly flowering perennials, such as rose mallow or gaillardia, should be cut back a good amount in the fall in order to sprout strongly again in spring and increase their lifespan.

Most perennials do not need a radical cutting back in the fall. On the contrary, fruits or grasses covered by hoarfrost are attractive even in winter. Only frost-sensitive plants, if not cut, resist cold better. If cut in the fall too early, the perennials have almost no opportunity to create reserves for the following year, so wait and cut them back in spring.

Those perennials whose young shoots lignify should be regenerated regularly. For instance, lavender and medicinal herbs are cut back considerably in early summer every two or three years.

Many groundcover perennials and evergreen perennials, e.g. thrift, do not need to be cut back every year. If fresh soil is applied to the bare places in the plant center and kept moist, new shoots will soon sprout again.

■ PLANT PROTECTION: Good locations and balanced nutrition keep the herbaceous plants healthy. Nevertheless, diseases caused by fungi, virus diseases or animal pests can appear - in particular, fading and stalk decay, gray mold fungi, mildew and rust. As for pests, greenflies, plant bugs, nematodes, mites, snails and slugs appear most frequently. Hares, rabbits and voles also like nibbling roots and shoots.

If the damage is small, try environmentally-friendly methods at first: Cut the infested places away, collect the pests, set traps or use plant infusions. Specialist stores offer a number of environmental and user-friendly preparations against heavier infestations. Herb preparations, which are often sold as ready preparations, are recommended because they make the plants stronger, thus protecting them from pests.

■ PLANT INFUSIONS: Fresh or dried plant parts are mixed with water, (4 pounds fresh and/or 1 pound of dried herbs per 5 gallons water – or proportionally), soaked one day and then boiled for half an hour. The mixture is then cooled in an uncovered pot, filtered and diluted 1:5 with water before use. Plant liquids must ferment for approximately two weeks until they do not foam any longer; they must also be mixed every day. Nettle liquid helps protect against greenflies, horsetail decoction against gray mold fungi, rust and scabies, and parsley fern tea against greenflies and spotted spider mites.

REPRODUCING PERENNIALS

▬ DIVIDING: Many perennials can be propagated easily and quickly this way. And since regeneration is necessary for most perennials, after several years, you can seize the opportunity! If the plant is too dense, the perennials hardly flower or bare places appear inside the plant, it is high time to propagate. At that point, the root ball can be eased out with a spade and divided with a small shovel. Perennials with fine fibrous roots should be divided by hand; fleshy rhizomes should be divided by means of a sharp knife. The young (daughter) plants should not be too small and should be replanted as soon as possible. The best time to do this is after the flowering period.

▬ SOWING: In spring, many perennials can be propagated by sowing in seed boxes placed in half-shade in the garden and kept evenly moist. A seedbed is also suitable. Most perennials can stand light frost during this period. In one or two months, the seedlings can be picked out and can be transplanted in the fall – or even better, in the following spring. Sowing is cheap, but requires patience and the new plants can vary in appearance, unlike the divided daughter plants.

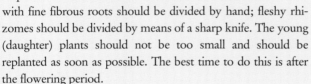

CREATION OF PERENNIAL BEDS

Despite the very wide variety offered, including many novelties, a bed for perennials must be created harmoniously and should not be overstocked. Otherwise, the soil will be exhausted and you will be disappointed with the bad growth and poor flowering. A drawing will enable you to plan precisely and help you to estimate the number of plants. You usually need 8 – 12 low perennials, 6 – 8 medium ones and 4 – 6 high ones per square yard. But these numbers are only a reference since every species and/or strain varies.

■ STRUCTURE: Trees and shrubs define the space, offer protection from weather influences and enhance the perennial bed in winter. They are the first to be planted. Those perennials able to stand shade, such as astilbe, foxglove, Japanese thimbleweed or bleeding heart, fit especially well in the transition zone between woody plants and bed perennials. Since bed perennials cannot stand strong rivals (e.g. of tree roots or shade), weak growing shrubs and roses should be their neighbors. A hedge or a wall can form a background for perennials, but a distance of 20 inches should be kept.

■ REPETITION AND HEIGHT GRADING: If you plant a species in larger or smaller groups, the bed is more harmonious. You can vary the number, distance and variety, and use various color shades so that the bed is not monotonous. The planting is more varied if you upgrade it with a few high central perennials, several medium ones and a lot of low accompanying ones and if high and medium perennials or grasses are occasionally given special emphasis. A uniform group will look "unnatural." Finally, the bed can be bordered by perennials with big leaves or perennials forming tufts. Flat perennial plants can be impressively diversified by individual or small groups of higher perennials.

■ CENTRAL PERENNIALS: These imposing figures often attract attention thanks to the beauty of their flowers; their flowering period is mainly the peak in the planting of perennials. They order and determine the character of the planting. We could name the following perennials as examples: high grasses, monkshood, plume poppy, delphinium, Sullivant's coneflower, eastern purple coneflower or foxtail lilies. Such an impressive perennial can also stand alone, e.g. next to the entrance or at a bend in a pathway, and it can put a special emphasis on the place.

Perennials with big leaves, such as bergenia, hosta, goatsbeard, Rodger's flower or giant rhubarb can be used as central perennials in shady areas because the big leaves do not dry so quickly there. But they need plenty of nutrients in order to thrive. They are decorative, even in winter. Light or varied leaves combined with light flowers can spotlight the darkest corner.

■ OBSERVATION OF FLOWERING PE-RIODS: Unlike annuals, perennials have a considerably shorter flowering period, but they often have more decorative foliage. When choosing plants, decide whether the flowering period will be in spring, summer or fall. If you combine your plants skillfully and if you plant spring flowers in the back part of the bed (so that the gap is not so striking after their flowering period), summer flowers in the center and fall flowers in front, you will enjoy your flowerbed all year round.

■ COLOR MATCHING: One or two colors of either flowers or leaves should dominate in a flowerbed and should contrast with the other color shades. Larger groups of harmonizing colors, e.g. yellow and red, are the most beautiful. White and blue flowers relax the whole. See to it that these color partners also flower simultaneously. Perennial beds planted in the shade attract attention to the form of the flowers. They make an impression if the plants flower simultaneously. In case of this variant, the flowering period lasts only several weeks at the most. If numerous colors are also complemented by a variety of flower forms, it has a disturbing effect. Therefore, use colors of the same variety. White has a neutralizing effect, whether in form of white flowers or white felted leaves.

FILLING IN GAPS: Quickly growing summer flowers, biennial spring flowers or bulb and tuber plants are often welcome "stopgaps" – whether at the beginning of planting when inter-plant gaps are still big, or in flowering breaks determined by individual seasons.

TIPS:

In large flowerbeds, keep small paths unplanted so as not to step on the perennials while caring for the plants.

Separate the lawn from the perennial bed using bordering stones so that the grass does not grow into the bed, saving yourself tedious digging.

Difficult areas in a garden, e.g. very dry or shady sites, can often be planted with wild perennials. They mostly have smaller flowers and a shorter flowering period than cultivated ornamental perennials, but they enchant with their natural charm. By the way, the term "wild" does not necessarily imply that they are indigenius to the area; it refers rather to their natural, not artificially processed form. Wild perennials are sensitive to excessive fertilization and dominant neighboring plants.

Bare places, e.g. under trees, can be planted very well with groundcovering perennials whose shoots or rhizomes spread quickly. They suppress weeds naturally and protect the soil from parching. Common periwinkle or hosta are suitable for the shade, common catnip and thyme form wonderful flower carpets in the sun.

This small encyclopedia cannot describe the complete variety of the world of perennials, but it is a good guide to some of the assortment available in stores. The following tips will help you to more easily reference the varieties which interest you.

The plants are listed in alphabetical order according to their botanical names.

Crossbreeds among varieties are marked with an "x" or with the word "hybrids." "Variety names" are in simple quotations marks.

The symbols in the box next to the text show you the most important characteristics of each plant. They have the following meaning:

Site:	Use:	Characteristics:
☀ Sun	**B** Beds and borders	➛ Groundcover
☀ Half-shade	**F** Free place	🪴 Pot plants
☀ Shade	**S** Rock garden	♫ Aromatic perennial
	G Woody plants and woody edges	✂ Cut perennial
	W Water/Bank	🌢 Winter protection
		! Poisonous and/or causing allergy

Some of the listed plants are poisonous or can cause allergies in sensitive people. Remember that children are often attracted by the flowers and fruits of poisonous plants, which frequently have marvelous colors. If in doubt, you should not plant that particular perennial.

Acaena buchananii
New Zealand burr

▬ FAMILY: *Rosaceae*

▬ ORIGIN: The blue-green New Zealand burr has its home in New Zealand.

▬ GROWTH: 2 – 4 inches high; the plant spreads through shoots covering the ground and has an average growth rate.

▬ FOLIAGE AND FLOWERS: Round, crenate, tripinnate leaves, rose-like; silver to gray-green at the top and bottom side evergreen. Rounded, plain flower head with green to yellow, cup-shaped needles. Flowering period is from June to July.

▬ SITE: Sunny, warm climate; in lighter, sandy, even dry soil. The plant cannot stand continuous waterlogging.

▬ USE: An evergreen groundcover suitable for smaller and larger places (10 – 20 plants or more), rock gardens, graves and roof gardens. Bulb flowers and grasses complement the plant cover impressively.

■ CARE NOTE: If the plant spreads too much, it can be cut. It tolerates dry seasons. It should be covered in winter in very cold regions.

■ PROPAGATION: It can be divided in spring or after flowering, sowed from the fall, preferably in frost-protected pots. In late spring, green shoots can be cut or rooted shoots can be eased out and planted.

■ SPECIAL CHARACTERISTICS: After flowering, striking red to red-brown, rounded-off, needle-shaped burrs appear; giving the plant its name.

■ OTHER VARIETIES: *A. microphylla* is distinguished by olive-green to brown foliage. The variety 'Kupferteppich' is more delicate than the variety and its brown-red foliage is impressive.

Acanthus hungaricus
Bear's Breeches

Site:
☼

Environment:
B S F

Characteristics:

■ FAMILY: *Acanthaceae*

■ ORIGIN: The Bear's Breeches, known as *A. longifolius* or *A. balcanicus*, comes from the Balkans.

■ GROWTH: Up to 40 inches high; bushy, upright, grows abundantly.

■ FOLIAGE AND FLOWERS: Up to 15 inches long, deeply lobed, very ornamental, dark green leaves. The white or light pink, lip-shaped flowers as well as the pink to crimson top leaves, sit on 25 – 30 inch long racemes. Flowering period is from July to August.

■ SITE: Sunny and warm climate; Loose, moderately dry, nutrient-rich soil.

■ USE: This imposing, wild perennial is suitable for beds and borders and stony areas such as rocky steppes. Its attractive shape, on its own or in small groups, stands out in sunny places or in front of a dark background. It is also suitable for containers or can be used as a cut flower.

CARE NOTE: It should be cut to the ground in winter, or in spring, and the rhizome should be covered. Potted plants are quite sensitive to the cold.

PROPAGATION: Divide in the fall or in spring, (the latter in cold regions), so that the plants will flower the following year. The variety can be sowed in spring or propagated through root shoots.

HISTORY: The ancient Greeks immortalized its ornate leaves on stone columns.

OTHER VARIETIES: The varieties of the *Acanthus Spinosissimus* group distinguish themselves by thorny, white-edged leaves.

Achillea filipendulina
Fern-Leaf Yarrow

Site:
☼

Environment:
B F

Characteristics:
↶ ✄ !

▬ FAMILY: *Asteraceae*

▬ ORIGIN: Caucasus, Orient; the varieties were often cultivated from hybrids of other varieties.

▬ GROWTH: 30 – 40 inches high; bushy and upright.

▬ FOLIAGE AND FLOWERS: Gentle, grayish green pinnate leaves with aromatic camphor-like scent. The numerous, golden yellow solitary flowers sit in big umbels. Flowering period is from June to November.

▬ SITE: Sunny, with fertile, nutrient-rich soil. No stagnant humidity – especially in winter.

▬ USE: Deep-colored, robust perennial; flowers for a long time; good for beds and borders, suitable as a cut or dried flower. It is nice on its own or in groups. Harmonious plant partners are blue and/or violet perennials, such as monkshood, larkspur, high clematis or sage varieties. A perfect plant for country gardens; attractive to bees.

CARE NOTE: Cut flowers last an especially long time if cut immediately after flowering. Cutting back the shoots which have just flowered encourages another blooming period in the fall.

PROPAGATION: The plant can be divided after flowering in spring or in the fall. Its flowering capacity will be preserved at the same time. It can be sowed in the fall or in spring.

SPECIAL CHARACTERISTICS: If touched, it can cause allergies.

VARIETY TIP: 'Parker' (45 inches) has golden yellow flowers, 'Coronation Gold' (30 inches) is a well-known hybrid variety with golden-yellow flowers flowering in November; 'Feuerland' has bright red flowers. All are nice as cut or dried flowers.

Achillea millefolium
Common Yarrow

━ FAMILY: *Asteraceae*

━ ORIGIN: Indigenous in Europe, Siberia and Asia; brought to North America, Australia and New Zealand.

━ GROWTH: 20 – 30 inches high, bushy and upright.

━ FOLIAGE AND FLOWERS: Gentle, fresh-green, oblong, pinnate leaves have a spicy scent. The white flowers with hints of red sit in umbrella-shaped umbels. The colored varieties show a color spectrum from yellow to carmine. Flowering period is from June to September or October, based on the climate.

━ SITE: This sun-lover prefers dry, nutrient-rich soil.

━ USE: An attractive flowering perennial for beds and borders; a suitable cut flower. It can be combined excellently with other perennials, e.g. bellflowers or sage. It is also attractive to bees.

━ CARE NOTE: The plant should be cut back after flowering and will sprout again quickly.

■■■ PROPAGATION: The plant can be divided after flowering in spring or in the fall. It can be sowed in the fall or in spring.

■■■ SPECIAL CHARACTERISTICS: The common yarrow is used as a styptic and disinfectant medicinal herb, thanks to a high content of essential oils and alkaloids. If touched, it can cause allergies.

■■■ VARIETY TIP: 'Crimson Beauty' and 'Fanal' have dark-red flowers, 'Lilac Beauty' is violet (all 25 inches high). 'Samme-triese' has velvet red flowers and is approximately 30 inches high.

Aconitum carmichaelii 'Arendsii'

Monkshood

▬ FAMILY: *Ranunculaceae*

▬ ORIGIN: Cultivation. The genuine variety has its home in China; the variety is also known as *A. x arendsii*.

▬ GROWTH: Up to 45 inches high; thick vegetation with strong, straight flower shoots.

▬ FOLIAGE AND FLOWERS: Big, deeply divided, hand-shaped, dark-green leaves. Violet racemes sprout from the ends of shoots. Flowering period is from September to November.

▬ SITE: Preferred half-shade, but sunny and shady places possible; in moist, fertile soil; the root area should be shaded. In case of humidity, diseases caused by verticillium spp. can appear easily.

▬ USE: An extraordinarily colored plant for shady, cold places. There it can be combined with other shade-loving partners such as ferns, anemones, astilbes, lilies or small coniferous trees. The cut perennial can be planted alone or in small

groups.

■ CARE NOTE: The plant should be cut back to the height of an upright hand after flowering.

■ PROPAGATION: The robust plant spreads through rhizomes which can be divided in early spring.

■ SPECIAL CHARACTERISTICS: Bumblebees love monkshood. However, it is poisonous to humans and other mammals. Wash your hands every time you touch this plant!

■ OTHER VARIETIES: *A. x cammarum* flowers have deep violet-blue flowers; the variety 'Bicolor' has blue and white flowers.

Ajuga reptans
Common bugle

Site:
☼ – ☀

Environment:
G W F

Characteristics:
〜〜➔

▬ FAMILY: *Lamiaceae*

▬ ORIGIN: The creeping common bugle originated in Europe and has spread to Asia Minor as well as to North Africa.

▬ GROWTH: 6 – 8 inches high; grows abundantly, with groundcover spreading through shoots.

▬ FOLIAGE AND FLOWERS: Obovate; the leaves of the variety are brownish red and shine metallically. Individual varieties have different leaves and flower colors. Small, whorl-shaped tubiform flowers in long spikes; violet blue. Many varieties are also white. Flowering period is from April to May.

▬ SITE: Bright (no full sun) to shady areas with fertile, moist soil.

▬ USE: The evergreen groundcover does well among, and in front of, woody plants as well as on pond banks. It is also suitable for greening open places. Neighboring perennials, such as ferns or grasses, make a nice combination.

▬ CARE NOTE: The plant needs a lot of space because it grows rampantly and strongly. The leaves falling in the fall can rot to a useful humus layer.

▬ PROPAGATION: Small rosettes can simply be separated from the groundcover in early fall or in spring. These varieties keep their color only through dividing.

▬ SPECIAL CHARACTERISTICS: The evergreen ground-cover provides protection to small animals in winter. The flowers are a popular nectar source.

▬ VARIETY TIP: 'Atropurpurea' has red leaves and blue flowers. The leaves of 'Burgundy Glow' are purple and white, those of 'Rainbow' are creamy white, red and green. 'Naumburg' and 'Schneesturm' have white flowers.

Alcea rosea
Rose mallow

■ FAMILY: *Malvaceae*

■ ORIGIN: The Chinese or common rose mallow has its home in Europe and has spread worldwide.

■ GROWTH: Up to 70 inches, strong, upright and bushy.

■ FOLIAGE AND FLOWERS: Big, heart-shaped, lobed leaf margin; dull green foliage. Pink, red or white flowers, single or double. Flowering period is from July to September.

■ SITE: Sunny and warm; fertile, loose, nutrient-rich soil.

■ USE: Imposing solitary plant for beds and borders, walls and fences or house entrances to which it lends a rural charm. Suitable as a cut flower as well. Monkshood or tall phlox are excellent companions.

■ CARE NOTE: Fertilization in spring promotes growth and flowering. Since the flowers grow very high, they appreciate support. Cut back before seed is released (or when you want to harvest the seed), in winter after flowering.

■ PROPAGATION: The perennial is most often planted as an annual or biennial plant. It is sowed in spring or in summer; young plants are picked out of pots later and replanted in the final site the following year.

■ VARIETY TIP: 'Nigra' has single, black-red flowers.

■ OTHER VARIETIES: *A. ficifolia* is hardier than *A. rosea* and is often available in a variety of colors.

Alchemilla mollis
Lady's mantle

▬ FAMILY: *Rosaceae*

▬ ORIGIN: The lady's mantle originates in the Caucasus and the Carpathian Mountains.

▬ GROWTH: 15 – 20 inches high; bushy, hemisphere-shaped, with strong expansion ability.

▬ FOLIAGE AND FLOWERS: Rounded, leaf margin slightly lobed, softly hairy, very decorative; dull green to grayish-green foliage. A large number of small, greenish-yellow solitary flowers sit in loosely structured panicles like a tender floral veil. Flowering period is from June to July.

▬ SITE: Sun to half-shade in looser, abundantly moist soil containing loam.

▬ USE: Ideal for borders, as a foreground for woody plants or along pond banks. It can also be used as high groundcover or as a decoration for bouquets. It can be planted on its own or in small groups (no more than 10); bergenias, forest bellflowers, high primroses or tall ornamental garlic are good companions for it.

■ CARE NOTE: The plant keeps its form if cut back near the earth after flowering, thus preventing it from losing too many seeds. Otherwise, it stands even when losing fall leaves.

■ PROPAGATION: It can be divided or sowed in spring or fall.

■ SPECIAL CHARACTERISTICS: The plant excretes "dew drops" at the leaf edges, glittering impressively in the sun. Popular nectar source for insects.

■ OTHER VARIETIES: *A. erythropoda* is smaller with a height of 4 inches. This variety is an ideal groundcover for sunny as well as shady areas and also grows well in dry soil.

Allium christophii
Star of Persia

Site:
☼

Environment:
B F S

Characteristics:
↻ ✄

▬ FAMILY: *Alliaceae*

▬ ORIGIN: The Star of Persia comes originally from Iran.

▬ GROWTH: 20 inches high; the bulb blooms with only one erect, round flower.

▬ FOLIAGE AND FLOWERS: Oar-shaped, spiked, up to 15 inches long; blue-green. The crimson, slightly metallic glittering star-shaped flowers sit in large, globular umbels that can reach an average of 8 inches. Flowering period is from June to July.

▬ SITE: Sunny and warm; the soil should be nutrient-rich, loose and dry rather than moist.

▬ USE: The ornamental flowers fit well in beds and borders or rock gardens. They can be cut or dried. New Zealand burr, witch's moneybags or grasses such as fescue are its best neighbors.

■ CARE NOTE: After the foliage has been drawn in, the overground plant parts can be cut back near the ground.

■ PROPAGATION: Parent bulbs should be planted or sowed in early spring.

■ SPECIAL CHARACTERISTICS: The whole plant smells of garlic. Since the leaves begin to yellow during the flowering period, it is best to put bulb flowers among other perennials.

■ OTHER VARIETIES: *A. aflatuense* impresses with globular, crimson umbels, *A. giganteum* is as much as 70 inches high. There are also smaller representatives, such as *A. moly*, which becomes wild easily and has yellow, umbrella-shaped umbels, or the well-known chive *(A. schoenoprasum).*

Anemone blanda
Greek thimbleweed

■ FAMILY: *Ranunculaceae*

■ ORIGIN: As indicated by the name, the Eastern Mediterranean region, the Balkans and Asia Minor are home to this anemone variety.

■ GROWTH: 4 – 6 inches high; the plant spreads intensively and creates thick colonies.

■ FOLIAGE AND FLOWERS: Trifoliate leaves, deeply lobed, crenate, they draw in after flowering; dark-green. The narrow, tongue-shaped petals sit around the flower center. They are star-shaped, and pink, red, blue or white. Flowering between March and April.

■ SITE: Half-shade; looser, fertile and moderately humid to dry soil.

■ USE: The plant prefers growing under green, deciduous, woody plants allowing sufficient light in spring. It likes northern sides or half-shaded areas of rock gardens. In bigger groups, it is quite hearty and suitable for bowls and containers.

■ PROPAGATION: The tubers can be divided after the flowering period. Fresh seeds can be sowed in summer.

■ VARIETY TIP: 'Atrocoerulea' has dark blue flowers; 'Blue Star' is light blue, 'Charmer' deep pink, 'Radar' violet-red with a white center, 'Violet Star' violet with a white center. The big, white flowers of 'White Splendour' are delicately pink on the underside.

■ OTHER VARIETIES: *A. nemorosa*, the native wood anemone, is suitable as a groundcover for shady places (the variety has white flowers; varieties are light blue to blue-violet).

Anemone hupehensis var. *japonica* 'Pamina'
Japanese thimbleweed

Site:
☀

Environment:
B G

Characteristics:
⚠

■ FAMILY: *Ranunculaceae*

■ ORIGIN: Cultivation. The variety (syn. *A. japonica*) comes from Japan and the south of China.

■ GROWTH: 10 – 12 inches high; bushy and compact – it spreads slowly through shoots.

■ FOLIAGE AND FLOWERS: Rounded to oval, deeply lobed; dull green. The bowl-shaped, semi-double, intensive pink flowers sit in loose panicles. Flowering period is from August to October.

■ SITE: Half-shade; in fertile, abundantly moist, nutrient-rich soil. The plant does not like damp and cold subsoil too well.

■ USE: For less sunny beds and borders, in front of and among woody plants, along northern walls, as a solitary or in small groups. Shade grasses and ferns, New Zealand burr, snakeroot or hostas are nice companions.

■ CARE NOTE: Japanese thimbleweeds do particularly well when supplied with sufficient nutrients and water. A light winter protection is generally advisable. If they are cut back to the ground in winter, they should be covered with the cut material or with brushwood. Late frost can be dangerous to young shoots.

■ PROPAGATION: The fibrous roots should be divided after the flowering period or in early spring. Sowing is possible, but it is best to propagate the varieties in a vegetative way.

■ SPECIAL CHARACTERISTICS: It is advisable, especially in the year of planting, to cover the plant as a protection against frost.

■ VARIETY TIP: 'Königin Charlotte' (40 inches, silver-pink, semi-double), 'Honorine Jobert' (40 inches, single, snow-white), 'Rosenschale' (30 inches, pink, red margins).

■ OTHER VARIETIES: Japanese thimbleweed, 'September Charme' *(A. hupehensis)*, has light violet-pink flowers.

Antennaria dioica 'Rubra'
Pussytoes

Site:
☀

Environment:
S F

Characteristics:
〜〜➤ ✂

■ FAMILY: *Asteraceae*

■ ORIGIN: Cultivation. The variety is native in Europe and has spread to Asia.

■ GROWTH: 4 inches high; flower shoots grow from a thick foliage carpet.

■ FOLIAGE AND FLOWERS: Fine, spatula-shaped; green on the top, silvery and felted on the bottom side. The carmine flower heads are arranged in corymbs which look like small cats' paws. Flowering period is from May to July.

■ SITE: Sunny and warm; in sandy, loose, poorer soil that could also be poor in calcium.

■ USE: A modest perennial for sunny and dry areas of a garden, especially rock gardens, wall cracks or free places of a heath nature. Good for graves or waysides. It creates thick, silver-foliage carpets and goes well with other plants, such as thyme, thrift or rock rose.

■ PROPAGATION: Division or separation of root shoots is easiest after flowering or in early spring. The variety can also be sowed.

■ SPECIAL CHARACTERISTICS: The flower heads attract butterflies magically; if dried, they can be added to bouquets.

■ VARIETY TIPS: 'Nyewoods' has deep pink flower heads.

■ OTHER VARIETIES: *A. dioica* var. *borealis* (syn. *A. tomentosa*) with fully silver foliage and white flowers.

Aquilegia vulgaris
European columbine

Site:
☼ – ☼

Environment:
B G

Characteristics:
✂ !

▬ FAMILY: *Ranunculaceae*

▬ ORIGIN: The European columbine is native to Europe; the wild form is protected.

▬ GROWTH: 25 inches high; upright, tufted.

▬ FOLIAGE AND FLOWERS: Deeply lobed, multi-divided, hairy, middle green or gray-green at bottom. Star-shaped flowers with short spurs are arranged in racemes; the variety has blue flowers, varieties are white, pink to red or deep violet, also double and without spurs. Flowering period is from May to June.

▬ SITE: The variety prefers half-shade, hybrid varieties also grow well in the sun. Fertile, abundantly moist, nutrient-rich soil is important.

▬ USE: For gaily colored perennial beds and borders, in front of and among loose, woody plants, and as a cut flower. Small groups are the most beautiful.

■ CARE NOTE: Cutting back after flowering prolongs its lifespan.

■ PROPAGATION: Sow after flowering (the varieties spread seeds easily by themselves). Varieties should be divided in spring or after flowering.

■ SPECIAL CHARACTERISTICS: The plant attracts bumblebees with its flowers. It is slightly poisonous to humans due to its prussic acid content.

■ VARIETY TIP: 'Black Barlow' (deep violet), 'Nivea' (white) and 'Nora Barlow' (pink-green) have striking, double flowers.

■ Other varieties: *A.-Caerulea-Varietye*, 'Crimson Star,' has bicolored flowers – red with a white bell. The mixture 'Mc Kana Hybrids' has many colors. The varieties *A. flabellata*, e.g. 'Ministar,' are different: they have blue-white flowers and are only about 8 inches high. They are suitable for rock gardens, pots and graves.

Armeria maritima 'Düsseldorfer Stolz'
Thrift

■ FAMILY: *Plumbaginaceae*

■ ORIGIN: Cultivation. The variety is found in the coastal areas of Northern Europe to Russia, Alaska and South America.

■ GROWTH: 8 inches high; upright flowers stand out from thick, spherical cushions.

■ FOLIAGE AND FLOWERS: Grass-like, oar-shaped leaves in thick rosettes; dark green, also in winter. Small, cup-shaped intensively carmine-pink flowers form spherical heads. Flowering period is from May to July, sometimes even longer.

■ SITE: Sunny; sandy, loose, or even stony soil or gravel, which can be acidic or neutral. Dryness is withstood better than humidity.

■ USE: A robust, modest perennial for sunny rock gardens which can grow in walls and grooves. It is suitable for heath gardens, and free, sunny slopes. Harmonious neighboring

Site:
☼

Environment:
S F

Characteristics:
 ✄

plants include alpine aster, pussytoes, grass pink or thyme. The perennial also does well in plant containers; its flowers grow in small bunches.

■ PROPAGATION: The plant can be divided easily from late summer to the fall or also in spring.

■ SPECIAL CHARACTERISTICS: The variety is protected because it forms a nesting place for waders. It offers plenty of nectar for insects.

■ VARIETY TIP: 'Alba' is white, 'Rotfeuer' is bright red.

■ OTHER VARIETIES: *A. juniperifolia*, only 2 inches high, is ideal for rock gardens and plant containers.

Artemisia 'Oriental Limelight'

Sage-brush

▬ FAMILY: *Asteraceae*

▬ ORIGIN: Cultivation. The variety is a hybrid of the usual Sage-brush (A. vulgaris); native to Europe.

▬ GROWTH: About 4 – 6 inches high, bushy, well-branched.

▬ FOLIAGE AND FLOWERS: Multiple pinnate leaves, evergreen; marked yellow-green.

▬ SITE: It prefers half-shade to full sun and loose, moderately dry soil.

▬ USE: Ornamental plant with decorative leaves for beds and plant containers. It is a good companion for many flowering plants, thanks to its varied foliage. Colorful young shoots have pretty foliage and bouquets.

▬ CARE NOTE: Shoots that become too long during summer and that make the plant shapeless can simply be cut back.

■ PROPAGATION: Varieties can be propagated only in a vegetative way, either by dividing in spring or in the fall, and/or through shoots in late summer or in spring.

■ SPECIAL CHARACTERISTICS: The perennial belongs to the "Proven Winners," i.e. the best varieties of the World Ornamental Plant Growers' Association. It is evergreen in temperate regions.

■ OTHER VARIETIES: *A. absinthium,* 'Lambrook Silver,' *A. arborescens,* 'Powis Castle,' as well as *A. ludoviciana,* 'Silver Queen' are very popular structurally due to their fine silver foliage (25 – 40 inches high). *A. schmidtiana,* 'Nana,' forms a 10 inch high foliage carpet and is also suitable for rock gardens (requiring a sunny place and sandy, dry soil).

Aruncus dioicus
Goatbeard

━ FAMILY: *Rosaceae*

━ ORIGIN: Native to Europe, it can also be found in East Asia and North America.

━ GROWTH: Up to 70 inches high; upright, bushy, well branched.

━ FOLIAGE AND FLOWERS: Big, pinnate leaves, up to 40 inches long, middle-green. The perennial is dioecious, i.e. there are plants with male cream-white flowers and plants with female pure white flowers. The flower panicles of the male plants are more impressive than those of the female and can even be 20 inches long. Flowering period is from June to July.

━ SITE: Half-shade to shade; fertile, moist, nutrient-rich soil.

━ USE: The ornamental goatbeard grows under high trees and fits in shady beds and borders. It is impressive, especially in front of evergreen coniferous woody plants. It can grow on its own or in groups; its companions can be astilbes, monkshood, foxglove, high bellflowers, hostas or ferns. The flowers can be used decoratively in vases.

■ CARE NOTE: Since the darkened flowers are still attractive in the fall and winter, the plant should be cut back near the earth in spring.

■ PROPAGATION: Divide and sow between late winter and early spring. The plant can set seed easily by itself.

■ SPECIAL CHARACTERISTICS: The leaves are slightly poisonous (prussic acid).

■ VARIETY TIP: 'Kneiffii' has cream-white flowers and is suitable for smaller gardens or containers because of its height of 30 inches.

Arundo donax 'Variegata'
Reed grass

Site:
☀

Environment:
W F

Characteristics:
🗑 ⚠

■ FAMILY: *Poaceae*

■ ORIGIN: Cultivation. The wild form is likely to come from Central Asia; however, it has spread from the Orient across the Mediterranean Sea to southern Europe.

■ GROWTH: Up to 80 inches high, higher in warm regions, the variety is 120 – 140 inches high; upright, reedlike, strong shoots, it spreads through creeping rhizomes.

■ FOLIAGE AND FLOWERS: Oblong, lance-like leaves, similar to bamboo, pendant; white-striped, dull gray-green. Feathery panicles do not appear in cold regions.

■ SITE: Sunny and warm; moist nutrient-rich soil.

■ USE: The imposing perennial can be planted on pond banks, but it also covers bare southern walls quickly. Its ornamental shape enhances every large garden. Sensitive to frost, but can be planted in a container in cool conservatories.

━ CARE NOTE: The thermophilic plant needs winter protection from frost: it should be bound together and covered with bamboo mats and brushwood; container plants must spend the winter in a cold, frost-free room. The plant should only be cut back in spring, and should be fertilized afterwards.

━ PROPAGATION: Separation of rhizomes from spring to early summer.

━ VARIETY TIP: 'Variegata Superba' is only 40 inches high and grows in width unrestrictedly.

Aster alpinus
Alpine aster

Site:
☼ – ☀

Environment:
S F

Characteristics:
🪣 ⛰

▬ FAMILY: *Asteraceae*

▬ ORIGIN: The asters are native to the European Alps and also grow in the mountains of Asia and North America. The wild form is protected.

▬ GROWTH: 8 – 10 inches high; bushy, compact cushions.

▬ FOLIAGE AND FLOWERS: Oblong to narrow spatula-shaped, medium-green foliage. The variety has white flowers; other varieties have violet and pink flowers. The tongue flowers are arranged as a star around the mostly yellow tubular flowers in the middle. Flowering period is from May to June.

▬ SITE: It prefers sun or half-shade; loose, but not too dry, limy or stony soil.

▬ USE: The compact perennial is ideal for rock gardens, dry walls, edges and larger plant containers. It can be planted on its own or in smaller groups.

■ CARE NOTE: The alpine aster tolerates semi-shaded places, but prefers sun. It should be divided every three years, and it should be cut back and mulched in the late fall in order to maintain its flowering intensity. If needed, the soil should be limed.

■ PROPAGATION: Divide in early spring or after the flowering period regenerates the plants.

■ SPECIAL CHARACTERISTICS: Popular as a nectar source – in particular among butterflies.

■ VARIETY TIP: 'Dunkle Schöne' has intensively violet flowers with a yellow center, 'Albus' is pure white and 'Happy End' is pink.

■ OTHER VARIETIES: The varieties of *A. tongolensis* are around 15 inches high; their flowers in violet shades appear from May to June. *A. amellus*, Ialian aster, is 20 – 30 inches high based on the variety and flowers in summer.

Aster novi-belgii
Aster

▬ FAMILY: *Asteraceae*

▬ ORIGIN: This variety is native to North America.

▬ GROWTH: 30 – 60 inches high based on the variety; upright, loosely bushy, the stalks are often reddish.

▬ FOLIAGE AND FLOWERS: Oblong, lance-shaped, smooth; dark green. The single to double flowers of the varieties are pink, red and blue. Blooming period is from September to October.

▬ SITE: Sunny, preferably cool; fertile, loamy, abundantly moist, nutrient-rich soil.

▬ USE: The high perennials are suitable for beds and borders, on their own or in small groups. They make beautiful cut flowers.

▬ CARE NOTE: The plant cannot tolerate a dry root ball. Especially high varieties need a support so as not to fall over.

Older, scattered plants are regenerated through dividing. The plant should be mulched after being cut back in the late fall.

■ PROPAGATION: Divide in early spring or after the flowering period.

■ SPECIAL CHARACTERISTICS: Popular nectar source for insects.

■ VARIETY TIP: 'Dauerblau' (blue-violet, long blooming period), 'Karminkuppel (striking carmine), 'Bonningdale White' (pure white, semi-double).

■ OTHER VARIETIES: New England asters *(A. novae-angliae)* and low asters *(A. dumosus)* flower in the fall as well.

Astilbe-Japonica-Hybride 'Europa'
Astilbe

■ FAMILY: Saxifragaceae

■ ORIGIN: Cultivation. The wild form of the astilbe comes from Japan.

■ GROWTH: 15 – 20 inches high; bushy, tufted.

■ FOLIAGE AND FLOWERS: Hand-shaped, compound, dark green foliage. The light violet-pink flowers form big, feathery panicles. Flowering between June and July, earlier than the other varieties.

■ SITE: Semi-shaded to shady, also sunny with sufficient humidity; fertile, moist, nutrient-rich soil, which should not dry out.

■ USE: The wild perennial likes the peripheries of woody plants, shady beds and borders or pond banks. Smaller varieties such as 'Europa' also grow in containers. A decorative cut flower.

■ CARE NOTE: The perennial should be divided every three or four years and old woody rhizomes should not be planted again.

■ PROPAGATION: Divide during the rest period in late winter.

■ SPECIAL CHARACTERISTICS: The flowers brown in the fall and remain attractive in winter as well. Cut them back in spring for this reason.

■ VARIETY TIP: 'Deutschland' (white), 'Mainz' (intensive violet pink), and 'Red Sentinel' (ruby, young leaves are purple).

■ OTHER VARIETIES: Astilbe *(A. x arendsii)* flowers with numerous colorful varieties from July to September (25 – 40 inches). Astilbe *(A. chinensis)* is approximately 15 inches high; its dwarf form *(A. chinensis var. pumila)* is only around 10 inches high. The latter also does well in the sun.

Bergenia-Hybrids
Bergenia

▬ FAMILY: *Saxifragaceae*

▬ ORIGIN: Cultivation. The varieties are native in particular to the Himalayas or in Kamtchatka.

▬ GROWTH: 8 – 20 inches high based on the variety; bushy, spreading through rhizomes, but not a rampant grower.

▬ FOLIAGE AND FLOWERS: Wide and round to heart-shaped, sturdy, wavy, green or reddish (often in the fall) foliage. Umbrella-shaped corymbs sit in fleshy peduncles; the color spectrum comprises white to pink and red variations. Flowering period is from April to May.

▬ SITE: Semi-shaded to shady, also sunny; moist, loose, nutrient-rich soil.

▬ USE: The evergreen foliage and flower perennial grows in front of and among woody plant groups, in shady borders as well as on banks; lower varieties also in rock gardens or in flower boxes. The leaves and flowers are a nice decoration for bouquets.

▬ CARE NOTE: Early flowers can be damaged by late frost. Withered leaves should be removed in early spring.

▬ PROPAGATION: Divide or sow in spring when rhizome cuttings are possible.

▬ VARIETY TIP: 'Abendglocken' (deep purple), 'Baby Doll' (tender pink, red flower stalk, fall coloring) 'Herbstblüte' (pink, it flowers again in the fall), 'Oeschberg' (pink with white, late flowering), 'Silberlicht' (white with a reddish eye).

▬ OTHER VARIETIES: *B. cordifolia* has dark red flowers. The green leaves get purple in the fall. The variety 'Purpurea' has purple flowers and red leaves.

Bistorta affinis
Himalayan fleeceflower

Site:
☼ – ☼

Characteristics:
F G S

Environment:
~~→

■ FAMILY: *Polygonaceae*

■ ORIGIN: This plant (syn. *Polygonum affine*) is native to the Himalaya in Nepal.

■ GROWTH: 10 inches high; forming thick cushions through shoots.

■ FOLIAGE AND FLOWERS: Oblanceolate leaves; fresh green, often red in the fall. Spiky, deep pink flowers stand out from the foliage carpet; the flowers get almost white when withering. Flowering period is from July to November.

■ SITE: Sunny to semi-shaded; loamy, moderately moist to wet, nutrient-rich soil rich in humus.

■ USE: A groundcover for the greening of slopes and larger free places in half-shade as well as in front of and among woody plants; also for rock gardens or graves. It is attractive if Japanese thimbleweeds, bergenias, common speedwell, hostas or grasses peer from the foliage carpet.

■ CARE NOTE: The modest perennial is suitable for areas that do not need much attention and care.

■ PROPAGATION: The plant is to be divided in spring; soft or half-ripe shoots should be cut from late spring to late summer.

■ SPECIAL CHARACTERISTICS: Intense reddish color in the fall.

■ VARIETY TIP: The flowers of 'Darjeeling Red' are pink at first and turn purple later. The bright pink 'Donald Lowndes' is only 6 inches high and does not grow so robustly, while the pink-red 'Superbum' grows rampantly and turns orange-red in the fall.

■ OTHER VARIETIES: The light pink flowers of *B. officinalis* (syn. *Polygonum bistorta*) grow up to 30 inches high. The variety prefers moist soil and likes growing on banks; the pink variety 'Superbum' does not grow rampantly.

Briza media
Quaking grass

Site:
☼ – ☼

Environment:
F S

Characteristics:
🪣 ✂

■ FAMILY: *Poaceae*

■ ORIGIN: Native to Europe, the grass also appears in southwestern Asia.

■ GROWTH: Approximately 15 inches high with the flowers; upright, loosely bush-like, finely divided.

■ FOLIAGE AND FLOWERS: Lineal, soft, up to 6 inches long, blue-green foliage. Tender heart-shaped spikes are arranged in loose panicles. Flowering period is from May to July.

■ SITE: Sunny to semi-shaded; sandy soil poor in nutrients.

■ USE: The modest grass is suitable for planting on sunny slopes as well as in stony and heath gardens. It can be planted well in groups or among other perennials and fits in bigger plant containers. Fescue varieties are harmonizing accompanying grasses. The dried, straw-colored panicles are popular.

■ CARE NOTE: The plant should be cut back in late winter.

▬▬ PROPAGATION: The plant should be divided in late spring or in early summer; annuals are sowed in spring at temperatures of approximately 50°F.

▬▬ SPECIAL CHARACTERISTICS: The plant is called "Quaking grass" because the spikes quake and rattle even in the gentlest wind.

▬▬ OTHER VARIETIES: The annual relatives are *B. maxima* and *B. minor*. The first one attracts attention with its 1 - 2 inch long, pendant, tear-like spikes. The other one is only about 10 inches high.

Calamagrostis x acutiflora
Feather reed grass

■ FAMILY: *Poaceae*

■ ORIGIN: This variety is native to Europe.

■ GROWTH: Foliage shrubbery approximately 25 inches high, with flowers up to 60 inches high; upright, bushy; spreads through rhizomes.

■ FOLIAGE AND FLOWERS: Narrow lineal, stiff, slightly pendant foliage. Yellow, narrow panicles. Flowering period is from July to August.

■ SITE: The plant loves the sun, but can also grow in light shade; moist to moderately moist, nutrient-rich soil.

■ USE: The strapping grass is impressive against a background of perennial beds and borders. It also looks nice in natural gardens or on the banks of lakes and ponds on its own or in groups; medium-sized perennials should be planted next to feather reed grass.

■ CARE NOTE: The flowers should be cut back in spring.

■ PROPAGATION: Divide from late spring to summer.

■ SPECIAL CHARACTERISTICS: The panicles are also decorative in winter, covered with hoarfrost or snow.

■ VARIETY TIP: 'Karl Foerster' is a wide grass with green leaves and bronze flowers. Unlike the variety, it does not grow rampantly (60 inches high with flowers). The green leaves of 'Overdam' have a yellow-white margin (50 inches high with flowers).

Campanula carpatica
Bellflower

■ FAMILY: *Campanulaceae*

■ ORIGIN: It is native to the Carpathian Mountains.

■ GROWTH: 8 – 12 inches high; bushy cushions.

■ FOLIAGE AND FLOWERS: Round to heart-shaped; intensely green foliage. Bell-shaped, blue or white flowers based on the variety. Flowering period is from June to August.

■ SITE: Sunny; moderately rich soil; not too dry, limy, or stony.

■ USE: The typical rock garden plant does well among stones, stairs and on dry walls. It can be planted as a narrow border or in front of flowerbeds. It grows well in bowls or flower boxes.

■ CARE NOTE: The perennials are frequently infested by snails and slugs. Therefore necessary measures should be taken.

■ PROPAGATION: Plants should be divided between late winter and early spring or shoots should be cut after flowering. They can be sowed in pots in the fall or in spring. The plants set seed abundantly.

■ VARIETY TIP: 'Blaue Clips' has light, violet-blue flowers; the white counterpart is 'Weiße Clips.' 'Blaumeise' has light blue flowers with white centers.

■ OTHER VARIETIES: *C. cochleariifolia* is only 4 inches high and has very delicate, white or blue flowers. The Dalmatian campanula *(C. portenschlagiana)* and *C. poscharskyana* form about 6 inch high cushions with stellate flowers in blue shades.

Campanula glomerata
Clustered bellflower

▬ FAMILY: *Campanulaceae*

▬ ORIGIN: Europe, Siberia and Central Asia.

▬ GROWTH: 15 – 20 inches high; bushy, spreading through shoots. The erect flower shoots are often reddish.

▬ FOLIAGE AND FLOWERS: Stalk leaves are oblong and lance-shaped, base leaves are egg-shaped to heart-shaped; all are dull green. The narrow, bell-shaped flowers form an end cluster, violet or white, based on the variety. Flowering period is from June to August.

▬ SITE: Sunny to semi-shaded; warm, limy, moderately moist, nutrient-rich soil.

▬ USE: The high variety is suitable for perennial beds and colorful borders; fits very well in front of woody plants and next to roses. It is used as a cut flower and for plant containers.

▬ CARE NOTE: The plant does not stand humidity well. If you do not want it to grow too abundantly, you must assign it

a limited space. Cutting back after the first flowering stimulates the second flowering period.

▬ PROPAGATION: Varieties are divided in early spring or shoots are cut after flowering. Varieties can be sowed in pots in fall or in spring; however, the plants spread abundantly on their own.

▬ VARIETY TIP: 'Dahurica' has dark violet whorls, 'Schneekrone' is pure white.

▬ OTHER VARIETIES: The peach-leaved campanula *(C. persicifolia)* is 30 – 40 inches high. The white or blue bell-shaped flowers (depending on the variety) sit in erect racemes.

Carex morrowii 'Variegata'
Sedge

Site:
☼ – ☀

Environment:
G W

Characteristics:

- FAMILY: *Cyperaceae*

- ORIGIN: Cultivation. The variety is native to Japan where it grows in marshlands.

- GROWTH: 12 inches high; widely tufted.

- FOLIAGE AND FLOWERS: Narrow, slightly bow-shaped pendant, dark green foliage with narrow, cream-colored stripes at the margin. Discreet yellow flowers sit on dark green spikes. Flowering period is from March to April.

- SITE: Semi-shaded to shady, high air humidity; loamy or sandy, fertile, moist soil.

- USE: The evergreen ornamental grass is a good choice for dark areas in front of or among woody plants or on pond banks. It harmonizes with rhododendrons. If planted in a container, it can stand on shady terraces, balconies or courtyards, but it should be protected from severe frost.

■ CARE NOTE: The perennial prefers places with high air humidity which are shielded from the wind.

■ PROPAGATION: Divide in late spring or early summer.

■ SPECIAL CHARACTERISTICS: Since the tufts are even beautiful in winter, do not cut the plant back until spring.

■ VARIETY TIP: 'Variegata Aurea' distinguishes itself by green, narrow leaves with a yellow stripe in the middle.

■ OTHER VARIETIES: *C. ornithopoda* 'Variegata,' sedge with white stripes, is only 8 inches high. Its leaves have a white stripe in the middle. On the other hand, leaves of *C. buchananii* are fuchsia-red (15 inches).

Centranthus ruber
Valerian

Site:
☼

Environment:
S F

Characteristics:

■ FAMILY: *Valerianaceae*

■ ORIGIN: The Red Valerian, as the variety is also called, comes from Alpine regions of Western and southern Europe.

■ GROWTH: 50 – 30 inches high based on the variety; branched in a bushy way, often woody. Its shoots are slightly nodding.

■ FOLIAGE AND FLOWERS: Wide lance-shaped, sturdy, blue-green foliage. The small, dark, pink-red funnel-shaped, solitary flowers sit in erect corymbs. It has a faint scent. Flowering period is from June to September.

■ SITE: Sunny and warm; dry to moderately moist, well-drained, limy or stony soil.

■ USE: The modest wild perennial is ideal for rock gardens and grows on dry walls as well. It does particularly well in front of warm southern walls. It can be planted on its own or on small groups. Its good companions are asters, fleabane, globe thistle or baby's breath. It is suitable for containers or vases.

■ CARE NOTE: If the withered flowers are removed regularly, the plant flowers again willingly. In winter, it is cut back to the ground and a light winter protection is recommended.

■ PROPAGATION: Divide in spring. The plants spread abundantly on their own if the location permits.

■ SPECIAL CHARACTERISTICS: The richly flowering Valerian is a popular nectar source for bees and other insects.

■ VARIETY TIP: 'Alba' is white, 'Coccineus' is raspberry-red.

Cimicifuga ramosa
Bugbane

▬ FAMILY: *Ranunculaceae*

▬ ORIGIN: This plant is native to the Asian peninsula of Kamtchatka

▬ GROWTH: Up to 80 inches high; upright, dense and bushy, tufted.

▬ FOLIAGE AND FLOWERS: Tripinnate leaves which are intensely green, often yellow in the fall. Tiny, white, solitary flowers form 15 inch stars, which nod gently and have a slightly unpleasant scent. Flowering period is from September to October.

▬ SITE: Semi-shaded to shady, cool, protected from wind; fertile, moderately to very moist soil rich in nutrients.

▬ USE: This impressive plant with the charm of a wild perennial grows well among woody plants. It looks very nice in front of conifers and makes every bare northern wall look better. Harmonizing neighboring plants include monkshood, Japanese thimbleweed, high bellflowers, ferns and shadow grasses.

■ CARE NOTE: The plant should be cut back near the ground and covered. Severe late frosts can damage young shoots.

■ PROPAGATION: Divide in early spring. Varieties can be sowed after flowering, but the seeds do not sprout easily.

■ VARIETY TIP: In case of 'Atropurpurea,' the purple bugbane, dark brown-red leaves contrast with white flowers.

■ OTHER VARIETIES: The *C. racemosa* flowers in summer, the *C. racemosa* var. cordifolia also flowers in the sun from August to October; the *C. simplex* flowers in the late fall.

Clematis integrifolia
Clematis

Site:
☼ – ☼

Environment:
F G

Characteristics:
✂

■ FAMILY: *Ranunculaceae*

■ ORIGIN: The clematis grows from Eastern Europe to Central Asia.

■ GROWTH: 25 inches high; not a climbing plant.

■ FOLIAGE AND FLOWERS: Egg-shaped, intensely green foliage. Nodding, solitary flowers are blue and grow up to 2 inches long; sepals are slightly turned. Flowering period is from July to August.

■ SITE: Preferably sunny, also semi-shaded; fertile, moderately moist, loose, nutrient-rich soil.

■ USE: The perennial grows in sunny areas in front of or among woody plants as well as in mixed flowerbeds. The flower shoots enhance colorful bouquets.

■ CARE NOTE: A support is advisable. The plant should be cut back to approximately 8 inches in the late fall, or in spring at the latest before sprouting.

■ PROPAGATION: Sow new seeds in the fall and cut shoots from spring to summer.

■ SPECIAL CHARACTERISTICS: Silvery-brown fruits (follicles) attract attention after flowering.

■ VARIETY TIP: 'Juuli' has bright blue-violet, star-shaped flowers. It flowers abundantly and is approximately 50 inches high.

■ OTHER VARIETIES: The best known clematis, *C. heracleifolia*, bewitches with pastel blue flowers. The flowers of 'Cassandra' are gentian-blue; those of 'Côte d'Azur' are light blue. The blue flowers of 'Campanile' have a distinct scent. The white *C. x jouiniana* 'Praecox' is a good groundcover alongside woody plants.

Convallaria majalis
Lily of the valley

■ FAMILY: *Convallariaceae*

■ ORIGIN: Native to Europe, protected.

■ GROWTH: 8 inches high; spreading through rhizomes, creating thick colonies.

■ FOLIAGE AND FLOWERS: Oblong, elliptic leaves; shine dark green, yellow in the fall and draw in early. The small, pendant, bell-shaped flowers sit in loose racemes and have a pungent odor. Flowering period is from May to June.

■ SITE: Semi-shaded to shady, not too cool; fertile, moderately moist, nutrient-rich (forest) soil.

■ USE: A charming groundcover for shady areas under trees and shrubs. It is also suitable for pots and bowls and the flowers are popular in small bouquets.

■ CARE NOTE: If the perennial grows too abundantly, it should be dug out in the fall or its growing area limited.

▬▬ Propagation: Divide after flowering. Sowing is possible, but the plant will not flower for several years.

▬▬ Special characteristics: Berries are formed after flowering; however, like the plant, they are poisonous.

▬▬ Variety tip: 'Grandiflora' has especially big, white flowers and is also suitable for a shady bed. 'Rosea' has light violet flowers and 'Albostriata' has cream-white, striped leaves. The double 'Flore Pleno' is rarer.

Coreopsis grandiflora 'Schnittgold'

Coreopsis

Site:
☼

Environment:
B

Characteristics:
✄

■ FAMILY: *Asteraceae*

■ ORIGIN: Cultivation. The coreopsis comes originally from southern regions of North America.

■ GROWTH: 30 inches high; loosely bushy.

■ FOLIAGE AND FLOWERS: Gentle, mostly pinnate, bright green leaves. Big, round, golden-yellow, cup flowers sit on wiry stalks. Flowering period is from June to September.

■ SITE: Sunny and warm; nutrient-rich, moderately moist, loose soil.

■ USE: The sunny color of this perennial has a place in every flowerbed and border. It is especially impressive in groups. The flowers, which can also be cut with buds, last for a long time in a vase.

■ CARE NOTE: The plant should be cut back to the ground in September in order to regenerate.

■ PROPAGATION: Divide after flowering or in spring. Then sow.

■ SPECIAL CHARACTER-ISTICS: Popular nectar source for bees and other insects.

■ VARIETY TIP: 'Early Sun-rise' attracts attention with semi-double, golden-yellow flo-wers (15 inches).

■ OTHER VARIETIES: The varieties of *C. lanceolata* are smaller and are suitable as border plants. The *C. verticillata* attracts attention with its needle-like, pinnate foliage and star-shaped flowers.

Cortaderia selloana
Cortaderia

▬ FAMILY: *Poaceae*

▬ ORIGIN: Argentina, Uruguay and south of Brazil.

▬ GROWTH: 80 to 120 inches high (with flower fans); erect, tufted.

▬ FOLIAGE AND FLOWERS: Narrow, sharply toothed at the margins, pendant, gray-green leaves. Up to 30-inch long, bushy, silver-white panicles sit on long, robust stalks. Flowering period is from September to November.

▬ SITE: Sunny, warm and protected; nutrient-rich, loose soil without humidity in winter.

▬ USE: The ornamental, evergreen grass grows in lawns or on pond banks. The flower fans are suitable for bouquets.

▬ CARE NOTE: Enough humidity in summer, fertilize once a month when watering. Frost protection in winter: bind the upper parts together and cover with pine branches or straw mats and mulch the root area. Cut back to 8 inches in spring.

▬ PROPAGATION: Divide in spring. Newly porchased plants are planted in spring.

▬ VARIETY TIP: 'Rendatleri' has gentle pink fans (80 inches), 'Argentea' and 'Sunnigdale Silver' have silver-white fans (80 – 100 inches). 'Pumila' is much smaller (50 inches).

Cyclamen hederifolium
Cyclamen

Site:
☀

Environment:
S G

Characteristics:
〜➡ 🔺

■ FAMILY: *Primulaceae*

■ ORIGIN: The variety is native in the Mediterranean region and is protected.

■ GROWTH: 4 – 6 inches high; upright, flowers and leaves shoot up from flattened tubers in the fall.

■ FOLIAGE AND FLOWERS: Heart-shaped, tipped leaves with a toothed margin resembling ivy. Nodding petals; pink flowers are markedly twisted. Flowering period is from (August) September to October – often before the leaves appear.

■ SITE: Semi-shaded and warm; loose, nutrient-rich and fertile, limy, dry to moderately moist soil.

■ USE: The small perennial is an ideal plant under woody plants. It grows in shady rock gardens as well. It is particularly impressive in groups.

■ CARE NOTE: In cold regions, it should be protected in winter. The flowers should be covered with pine branches – loosely.

■ PROPAGATION: Fresh, ripe seeds should be sowed in midsummer. The plant spreads by itself, forming small, thick colonies. Tubers should be planted approximately 2 inches deep in the fall and should be covered with leaves or pine branches during winter.

■ VARIETY TIP: 'Album' has white flowers.

■ OTHER VARIETIES: The *C. coum* has bright pink flowers from February to April.

Delphinium grandiflorum
Delphinium

■ FAMILY: *Ranunculaceae*

■ ORIGIN: Western China and Siberia.

■ GROWTH: 12 – 20 inches high, based on the variety; bushy, compact.

■ FOLIAGE AND FLOWERS: Hand-shaped, deeply lobed; fresh green leaves. Cup-shaped, gentian-blue flowers. Flowering period is from June to August.

■ SITE: Sunny; loose, sandy-loamy soil.

■ USE: A unique touch for beds, borders, rock gardens, pots and bowls. It is also nice in bouquets of summer flowers.

■ CARE NOTE: The perennial cannot stand humidity or frost. If it is cut back directly after flowering, it flowers for a second time in the fall. It should be covered in winter or sowed every year in cold regions.

■ PROPAGATION: Sow in early spring. High delphiniums (apart from Pacific-Hybrids) are propagated through dividing or shoots.

■ SPECIAL CHARACTERISTICS: If touched, the leaves can cause skin irritation. The flower is attractive to bumblebees.

■ OTHER VARIETIES: The high delphiniums flower from June to July and again in September-October, after you cut them back. *D.-Belladonna*-Hybrids grow up to 50 inches high. There are blue, violet and white varieties. *D.-Elatum*-hybrids grow to 80 inches or even higher. There are violet, blue, pink and white varieties. A particularly striking variety is *D.-Pacific*-hybrid, 'Black Night,' which has dark violet flowers (70 inches).

Dianthus plumarius 'Maggie'
Grass pink

■ FAMILY: *Caryophyllaceae*

■ ORIGIN: Cultivation. The variety comes from South-eastern Europe and is protected.

■ GROWTH: 8 – 12 inches high based on the variety; creating thick cushions.

■ FOLIAGE AND FLOWERS: Narrow, grass-like, spiked, blue-green foliage. Round, deeply lobed; "feathery" appearance; fragrant; dark pink flowers. Other varieties are white or red. Flowering period is from June (July).

■ SITE: Sunny and warm; well-drained, limy, moderately dry soil.

■ USE: An evergreen perennial for rock gardens and dry walls, edges and plant boxes. Also suitable as a cut flower.

■ CARE NOTE: The demanding plant does not like continuous (soil) humidity.

Site:

Environment:
S

Characteristics:

▬ PROPAGATION: Varieties are propagated by dividing, preferably in the fall or in early spring.

▬ SPECIAL CHARACTERISTICS: Butterflies like the flowers of the grass pink.

▬ VARIETY TIP: 'Alba Plena' and 'Diamant' have white double flowers; 'Heidi' has red double flowers, 'Doris' is salmon-pink with a red center, 'Munot' has deep-red double flowers.

▬ OTHER VARIETIES: There are red and white varieties of the maiden pink *(D. deltoides)* suit-

able for rock and heath gardens. The foliage cushion of *D. gratianopolitanus* is dotted with pink, red or white flowers (based on the variety). 'Blaureif' attracts attention with its silver-blue foliage. The violet-pink flowers of *D. amurensis* bloom from June to September.

Dicentra spectabilis
Bleeding heart

Site:
☀

Environment:
G B

Characteristics:

■ FAMILY: *Fumariaceae*

■ ORIGIN: The natural habitats for this plant are in China and Japan.

■ GROWTH: 25 – 30 inches high; bushy, spreading through rhizomes.

■ FOLIAGE AND FLOWERS: Fern-like; blue-green leaves turn yellow and draw in in summer. White, internal petals look like tears falling from heart-shaped, pink flowers. The flowers sit in bow-shaped racemes. Flowering period is from May to June.

■ SITE: Semi-shaded; fertile and nutrient-rich, moderately damp, loose, acidic soil.

■ USE: The plant fits particularly well in the shade of woody plants, such as rhododendrons, in semi-shaded borders or on bare northern walls. It is a traditional choice for country gardens and also does well in containers. The racemes are suitable for vases.

■ CARE NOTE: The plant does not like stagnant humidity. Late frosts can be dangerous for young shoots.

■ PROPAGATION: Rhizomes are divided in late winter or shoots are cut in summer.

■ SPECIAL CHARACTERISTICS: The perennial draws in shortly after flowering. That is why it is best to combine them with other "shade perennials" or ferns.

■ VARIETY TIP: 'Alba' has pure white flowers.

■ OTHER VARIETIES: The wild bleeding heart *(D. eximina)* is only about 8 inches high. Its flowers are pink-red; the flowers of the variety 'Alba' are white. They appear from May to July. A specialty is *C. formosa* 'Stuart Boothman' with damask-colored flowers over fine, gray-green leaves (12 inches).

Digitalis purpurea
Purple foxglove

Site:
☀ – ☀

Environment:
G B F

Characteristics:
✄ !

━ FAMILY: *Scrophulariaceae*

━ ORIGIN: The purple foxglove is native to Europe where it is often found in glades.

━ GROWTH: 60 inches high; upright, basal leaf rosette.

━ FOLIAGE AND FLOWERS: Narrow, oblong or egg-shaped, dark green leaves. Big bell-shaped, solitary flowers sit in long, thick racemes; they are lilac (red), pink or white based on the variety. Flowering period is from June to July.

━ SITE: Semi-shaded, also sunny; fertile, dry soil which is poor in lime.

━ USE: The evergreen foxglove looks lovely among woody plants, such as rhododendrons, and it fits into natural gardens harmoniously. High bellflowers, goatbeard, snakeroot, wild grasses and ferns complement this plant. It is also suitable for beds and borders as well as heath gardens.

▬ CARE NOTE: Cut back after flowering.

▬ PROPAGATION: The culture is mostly biennial, so it is sowed in early spring. The plant also sets seeds abundantly.

▬ SPECIAL CHARACTERISTICS: The perennial contains poisonous glycosides that are used in heart medication. Bumblebees like it as a nectar source.

▬ VARIETY TIP: 'Gloxiniaeflora' with lilac-red flowers and 'Gloxiniaeflora Alba' with white flowers are well-known. 'Excelsior' has purple, pink and white flowers. 'Suttons Apricot' attracts attention with its salmon-pink flowers.

▬ OTHER VARIETIES: The yellow foxglove *(D. lutea)* loves lime and has lemon-yellow flowers.

Dryopteris filix-mas
Male fern

Site:
☀ – ☀

Environment:
G W

Characteristics:
 !

■ FAMILY: *Dryopteridaceae*

■ ORIGIN: The common male fern, indigenous to Europe, is now widespread across the northern hemisphere to South America.

■ GROWTH: Up to 40 inches high; upright, funnel-shaped, tufted.

■ FOLIAGE: Simple pinnate, broad, soft, feathery fronds; dull green.

■ SITE: Shady to semi-shaded, cool; in moist, fertile (wood) soil.

■ USE: This fern is suitable for all the shady parts of a garden where it grows best in front of or among woody plants. It can be grown on graves or in containers and near ponds. It is most impressive as a solitary plant due to its size.

■ CARE NOTE: The fern prefers growing without disruption, in sunny places with sufficient moisture. The soil can be prepared with farmyard humus or foliage soil.

■ PROPAGATION: Divide in spring.

■ SPECIAL CHARAC- TERISTICS: The male fern, which was used as a medi- cine against tapeworms, is poisonous.

■ VARIETY TIP: 'Bar- nesii' grows steeply upright (30 – 40 inches) with slight-

ly waved, feathery fronds. The male fern variety, 'Linearis Poly- dactylon' (20 – 30 inches high), has long, very curly fronds with narrow, lobed, pinnate leaflets whose ends grow bushily together.

■ OTHER VARIETIES: *D. affinis* has deep-green fronds with golden-brown scaly stalks, which are very contrasting. In regions with temperate climate it is evergreen. *D. dilatata* has very wide tripinnate fronds. *D. wallichiana* attracts attention with black, scaly frond petioles and lateral veins.

Echinacea purpurea
Eastern purple coneflower

Site:
☼

Environment:
B F

Characteristics:
🗑 ✂ !

▬ FAMILY: *Asteraceae*

▬ ORIGIN: Eastern purple coneflower *(syn. Rudbeckia purpurea)* comes from the dry regions of North America.

▬ GROWTH: 40 inches high; upright, branched in a bushy way.

▬ FOLIAGE AND FLOWERS: Lance to egg-shaped, sharply incised margin, sturdy, leather-like and rough haired, deep green foliage. Radial purple, stellate flowers are distributed around a high arched center of brown-red tubular flowers. Flowering period is from June to September.

▬ SITE: Sunny; fertile and nutrient-rich, loose and limy soil.

▬ USE: The perennial gives flowerbeds and borders a special color. It is suitable for containers and also as a cut flower.

▬ CARE NOTE: If the withered anthodia are cut, new ones appear right away. The perennial should be cut back to the ground in spring.

■■ PROPAGATION: Sow or divide (varieties) in spring. If you want to reap the roots in the late fall/winter, you can propagate root cuttings.

■■ SPECIAL CHARACTERISTICS: The eastern purple coneflower is a well-known medicinal herb. Many medical products are produced mainly from the roots, but they can have an allergic effect on sensitive persons. Bees and other insects enjoy its nectar.

■■ VARIETY TIP: 'Abendsonne' has salmon-carmine flowers, the pink flowers of 'Magnus' are big and hearty. 'Alba,' 'White Lustre' and 'White Swan' have white flowers with orange centers.

Echinops ritro
Globe thistle

▬ FAMILY: *Asteraceae*

▬ ORIGIN: In rocky, stony areas of southern Europe and the Balkans.

▬ GROWTH: 40 – 60 inches high; bushy, upright.

▬ FOLIAGE AND FLOWERS: Deeply lobed, incised leaf margin; leaves are blue-green on the top, white-felted on the bottom side. The pompon flower heads are an extraordinary, sparkling steel-blue; the buds have a metallic glimmer. They grow from robust, gray-felted stalks. Flowering period is from July to September.

▬ SITE: Sunny, warm; well-drained, dry soil.

▬ USE: For sunny beds and slopes or natural gardens; nice as a cut or dried flower.

▬ CARE NOTE: The plant does best in dry sites and does not endure winter humidity especially well. It should be cut back after flowering or in spring.

■ PROPAGATION: Divide in fall or in early spring; sow in spring.

■ SPECIAL CHARACTERISTICS: Very robust and hardy. Popular with bees and butterflies.

■ VARIETY TIP: 'Veitch's Blue,' with steel-blue flower heads over gray foliage, is a bit smaller than the variety (30 – 40 inches). It is a popular cut flower.

■ OTHER VARIETIES: *E. bannaticus* 'Taplow Blue' has violet-blue flower heads.

Eryngium alpinum distinguishes itself with violet, thistle-like flowers.

Epimedium x rubrum
Barrenwort

Site:

Environment:
G

Characteristics:

■ FAMILY: *Berberidaceae*

■ ORIGIN: Cultivation. A hybrid of the woodland wind-flower *E. grandiflorum* and the *E. alpinum*.

■ GROWTH: 12 inches high; bushy, the perennial spreads through rhizomes.

■ FOLIAGE AND FLOWERS: Double trifoliate foliage, with egg-shaped, spiked leaflets with prickly-toothed margins; gently reddish at first, intensely red to red-brown in the fall. The small, spur-shaped flowers are carmine and yellowish-white internally. They sit in loose racemes. Flowering period is from April to May.

■ SITE: Semi-shaded to shady; in fertile and nutrient-rich, moist, but well-drained soil.

■ USE: The wild perennial is ideal for bare places under trees and shrubs because it even grows in soil full of roots.

■ CARE NOTE: If the older leaves are removed, the younger ones dramatically change color in the fall. The plant should be cut back to the earth in late winter. Since the frost can damage the above ground plant parts, it is advisable to plant it in a wind-protected place and cover it with a mulch cover.

■ PROPAGATION: Divide in late winter or after flowering. You can get rhizome cuttings (about 2 – 3 inches long) in the fall and in winter. Let them take root at home and plant them after the frost period.

■ OTHER VARIETIES: *E. grandiflorum* 'Rose Queen' has deep pink flowers; 'Elfenkönigin' is cream-white. *E. x versicolor* 'Sulphureum'attracts attention with sulphur-yellow flowers and a bright brown color in the fall. The flowers of *E. x warleyense*, 'Orange Königin,' are striking orange.

Eremurus stenophyllus
Foxtail lily

▬ FAMILY: *Asphodelaceae*

▬ ORIGIN: The foxtail lily (syn. *E. bungei*) grows in the wild in West and Central Asia.

▬ GROWTH: 30 – 40 inches high; tufted, the fleshy roots spread in a starfish-shaped manner.

▬ FOLIAGE AND FLOWERS: Oar-shaped, blue-green basal leaves die off after flowering. The small, bright yellow, solitary flowers sit in long, candle-shaped racemes. Flowering period is from June to July.

▬ SITE: Sunny and warm, they should be protected from humidity; nutrient-rich, deep, loose, dry soil.

▬ USE: The imposing plant can be a central plant in a flowerbed and borders. It is also suitable for rock gardens. It can be planted on its own or in small groups. Since the leaves draw in at the end of the flowering period, the foxtail lily should have some companions, such as ornamental grasses. The flowers can be put in a vase.

■■ CARE NOTE: It is recommended to add a 1 to 2 inch thick sand layer to the soil, in particular if the soil is firm. The fragile roots are planted carefully approximately 6 to 8 inches deep. The plant should be protected from humidity and frost in winter.

■■ PROPAGATION: Division of plants or sowing of fresh seeds can be done after flowering.

■■ OTHER VARIETIES: *E. x isabellinus* 'Ruiters-hybrids' grow up to 30 inches high. They have yellow, orange, pink, red or white flowers based on the variety. *E. robustus* is approximately 90 inches high. The racemes with their pink buds and white flowers show an extraordinary interplay of color.

Erigeron-Hybrid *'Adria'*
Fleabane

■ FAMILY: *Asteraceae*

■ ORIGIN: Cultivation. The variety is a hybrid of the North American wild variety, *E. speciosus*.

■ GROWTH: 25 inches high; densely branched.

■ FOLIAGE AND FLOWERS: Lance-shaped, gray-green, basal leaves. The fine, dark blue, stellate tongue flowers sit on aster-like flower heads. Flowering period is from July to August, the second flowering period is in August-September.

■ SITE: Preferably sunny, also semi-shaded; nutrient-rich, well-drained soil.

■ USE: An abundautly flowering perennial for beds and borders; excellent as a cut flower. The intense flower colors contrast strikingly with a backround of dark woody plants. Balcony owners can use it as a container plant.

■ CARE NOTE: If the plant is cut back short, just above the ground, after its main flowering, it will flower lavishly again in late summer. Fertilization in early spring promotes sprouting.

■ PROPAGATION: Divide from spring to summer. Cut green shoots in spring. Dividing every three or five years ensures the regeneration of the plant.

■ VARIETY TIP: 'Dunkelste Aller' has deep violet flowers; 'Rotes Meer' is dark red. The white flower heads of 'Sommerneuschnee' have a pink tinge.

■ OTHER VARIETIES: The *E. karvinskianus* is approximately 12 inches high and is suitable for flower boxes and hanging pots or baskets as well as for rock gardens. However, it is not quite so hardy.

Eupatorium cannabinum
Hemp agrimony

■ FAMILY: *Asteraceae*

■ ORIGIN: The variety is native in Europe and can also be found in North Africa and Central Asia. It is well-known as holy rope or St. John's Herb.

■ GROWTH: 50 inches high; stalks are upright, reddish and sparsely branched; it spreads in tufts.

■ FOLIAGE AND FLOWERS: Oblong, egg-shaped, spike-shaped foliage; four deep green leaves sit in whorls on a stalk. Thick, salmon-pink umbels release a pleasant scent. Flowering period from July to September.

■ SITE: Sunny to semi-shaded; in nutrient-rich, loamy, moist soil.

■ USE: This perennial prefers banks of ponds or rivers with sufficiently moist soil. It looks nice bordering woody plants. It is best to plant it on its own. The umbels last for a long time both in the garden and in a vase.

■ CARE NOTE: Cut low, close to the ground in late winter or in spring.

■ PROPAGATION: Sow in spring or divide before growth begins.

■ SPECIAL CHARACTERISTICS: The huge umbels, rich in nectar, are often visited by bees, bumblebees and butterflies.

■ OTHER VARIETIES: *E. purpureum* 'Atropurpureum' (syn. *A. fistulosum*) is 70 inches high. The purple stalks attract attention next to wine-red flowers. The wine-red 'Purple Blush' is 55 inches high. *E. rugosum* 'Chocolate' (*Ageratina altissima* now) is distingushed by brown leaves and white flowers (40 inches).

Euphorbia polychroma
Cushion spurge

■ FAMILY: *Euphorbiaceae*

■ ORIGIN: The cushion spurge comes from southeastern Europe.

■ GROWTH: 12 – 16 inches high; richly branched, tufted, spreading through its branched rhizome.

■ FOLIAGE AND FLOWERS: Narrow, lance-shaped, lightly haired foliage which is dark green and turns strikingly red in the fall. The tiny leaves are surrounded by bright yellow bracts and sit in umbrella-shaped flowers. Flowering period is from May to June, but the color of the bracts lasts longer.

■ SITE: Sunny and warm; in moderately dry, loose, limy soil.

■ USE: The sun lover is suitable for greening slopes and enhancing borders. It loves the warmth of southern walls and enriches every rock garden.

Site:
☼

Environment:
B F S

Characteristics:
⌇⌇⟶ !

■ PROPAGATION: Divide or cut shoots in spring after flowering. Sowing is possible in the fall or in spring.

■ SPECIAL CHARACTERISTICS: The cushion spurge contains a poisonous, milky juice which flows from the plant if it is even slightly injured. This can be dangerous for small children and pets. It is recommended to use gloves when handling this plant because the juice can irritate the skin.

■ VARIETY TIP: The 'Purpurea' is distinguished by a combination of light yellow bracts and reddish leaves.

■ OTHER VARIETIES: The *E. myrsinitis* creates thick cushions full of light yellow umbels. The rock garden perennial grows well on dry walls.

Festuca glauca
Festuca

▬ FAMILY: *Poaceae*

▬ ORIGIN: This grass grows naturally across southeastern France and northwestern Italy.

▬ GROWTH: 8 inches high (with flowers 15 inches); spherical tufts, does not grow lavishly.

▬ FOLIAGE AND FLOWERS: Narrow, grass-like, evergreen; gray-blue to blue-green. The flowers sit in blue-green, later light brown, panicles. Flowering period is from June to July.

▬ SITE: Sunny and warm; nutrient-rich, loose, dry, and also limy soil.

▬ USE: A compact grass for rock gardens, stone grooves and gravel beds. Several plants quickly form a green carpet. The evergreen perennial is also suitable for borders as well as for containers and graves.

▬ CARE NOTE: If the flowering panicles are removed, the foliage tufts turns a vivid color.

▬ PROPAGATION: Divide in spring. The plant spreads abundantly in a favorable place.

▬ VARIETY TIP: The 'Frühlingsblau' has steel-blue leaves and the 'Glaucantha' is only 4 inches high. The 'Silbersee' is special with its silvery-white stalks.

▬ OTHER VARIETIES: The *F. mairei* is much taller, at 25 inches. Its narrow gray-green leaves hang slightly and are also nice in winter.

Filipendula rubra
Meadow sweet

Site:
☼ – ☀

Environment:
W B

Characteristics:

■ FAMILY: *Rosaceae*

■ ORIGIN: This plant comes from North America where it is known as "Queen of the Prairie."

■ GROWTH: 60 inches high; loosely upright, tufted.

■ FOLIAGE AND FLOWERS: Irregularly cut lobes, individual leaves double-dented at the margin and wrinkled. The small, rose-colored flowers sit in feathery plumes. Flowering period is from July to August.

■ SITE: Sunny to semi-shaded; fertile, loamy, moderate to moist soil.

■ USE: A solitary perennial for banks of ponds, rivers and marshy places. It also grows abundantly in moist flowerbeds and borders.

■ PROPAGATION: Varieties are divided in spring or propagated through shoots until summer. Varieties can be sowed in spring too.

■ SPECIAL CHARACTERISTICS: The pleasant-smelling flowers are followed by brownish fruit.

■ VARIETY TIP: The 'Venusta' sparkles with pink-red panicles. The deep red 'Nana' is very compact with its height of 12 inches.

■ OTHER VARIETIES: *F. vulgaris* 'Plena' captures attention with its white, double flowers. It is only 15 inches high. It likes dry, sunny places such as rock gardens, and makes a beautiful cut flower.

Fragaria-Hybride 'Pink Panda'

Strawberry

Site:
☀ – ☀

Environment:
G

Characteristics:
〰→

▬ FAMILY: *Rosaceae*

▬ ORIGIN: Cultivation: This variety is a hybrid of the Woodland strawberry *(F. vesca)* and potentilla.

▬ GROWTH: 4 – 6 inches high; creates thick carpets.

▬ FOLIAGE AND FLOWERS: Dark green, evergreen foliage with slighly silver-haired leaves with jagged margins. Pink, saucer-shaped flowers. Flowering period is from June to September.

▬ SITE: Semi-shaded and cool, also sunny; nutrient-rich fertile, sandy loamy, moist soil.

▬ USE: The strawberry is a multipurpose plant. It quickly greens bare areas as a evergreen groundcover under trees and shrubs. Additionally, it is suitable for borders and graves. You can plant it in flower boxes or hanging pots and baskets on your balcony or terrace.

■ CARE NOTE: An organic fertilizer used in spring promotes the growth of this plant.

■ PROPAGATION: Strawberries can be propagated through shoots from summer to the fall. They take root in the earth or in pots.

■ SPECIAL CHARACTERISTICS: Small red, very tasty 'fruit' appear after flowering.

■ VARIETY TIP: The 'Rumba' has sparkling pink flowers; the 'Samba' has dark-pink flowers.

■ OTHER VARIETIES: If you like colorful leaves, you should choose the strawberry 'Variegata' *(F. vesca)* with its green-white leaves.

Gaillardia x grandiflora 'Kobold'
Gaillardia

▬ FAMILY: *Asteraceae*

▬ ORIGIN: Cultivation. The plant originally comes from North America.

▬ GROWTH: 8 – 10 inches high; bushy; compact.

▬ FOLIAGE AND FLOWERS: Basal leaves are mostly pinnate; bright green stalk leaves are oblong and hairy. Large flowers: anthodiums with red petals tipped with yellow and dark red tubular flowers in the middle. Flowering period from July to September.

▬ SITE: Sunny and warm; fertile, sandy loamy, well-drained, moderately moist soil.

▬ USE: A colorful plant for beds and borders; perfect in sunny areas in the foreground of dark woody plants. It is a good companion for fleabane, coreopsis, delphinium, eastern purple coneflower or sage. Suitable for plant containers and higher varieties make good cut flowers as well.

■ CARE NOTE: The perennial needs to be fertilized regularly during the flowering season in order to flower luxuriantly the following year. It should be cut back after flowering and covered with pine branches in winter.

■ PROPAGATION: Individual, rooted shoots should be divided or sowed in spring.

■ SPECIAL CHARACTERISTICS: The perennial is not long-lived; however, it flowers the whole summer.

■ VARIETY TIP: The 'Bremen' has also red and yellow flowers; the 'Burgunder' is wine-colored. The 'Fackelschein' is a mixture of red and yellow flowers. The above mentioned varieties are 20 – 25 inches high and are particularly popular cut flowers.

Galanthus nivalis
Common snowdrop

▬ FAMILY: *Amaryllidaceae*

▬ ORIGIN: The common snowdrop is native to Central and southern Europe and is protected. Wild plants can be found even in the Caucasus.

▬ GROWTH: 6 inches high; two or three leaves develop from every bulb; the plant spreads quickly by dropping seed and parent bulbs and creates thick colonies.

▬ FOLIAGE AND FLOWERS: Slender, lineal, up to 8 inches long, it draws its blue-green foliage in shortly after flowering. One white, bell-shaped flower hangs on every stem; each flower has green tinged inner petals. Flowering period from February to March.

▬ SITE: Semi-shaded, cool; fertile, moist soil.

▬ USE: The snowdrops announce the spring, whether in a garden, as a potted plant or in small bouquets. They also form thick, large flower carpets under woody plants.

■ CARE NOTE: This small perennial prefers being left in peace. It is planted approximately 4 inches deep in late summer or fall.

■ PROPAGATION: Large groups should be divided after flowering when the foliage is still green. Available parent bulbs can then be easily removed. You can collect the seeds or wait until the plant sets seed by itself.

■ SPECIAL NOTES: All parts of the plant are slightly poisonous; indigestion can result from consumption; the skin can be irritated after contact with the bulbs.

■ VARIETY TIP: 'Plenus' has double flowers.

■ OTHER VARIETIES: *G. elwesii*, the giant snowdrop, flowers a bit earlier and grows in dryer soil too, in a rocky garden for example.

Gentiana sino-ornata
Gentiana

▬ FAMILY: *Gentianaceae*

▬ ORIGIN: western China.

▬ GROWTH: 6 inches high; it forms thick, lawn-like cushions through low shoots.

▬ FOLIAGE AND FLOWERS: Slender, lineal, spiked, fresh green foliage. The azure blue, trumpet-shaped flowers sit individually on the ends of the arching stems. The petals are striped yellow-green. Flowering period is from September to October.

▬ SITE: Sunny to semi-shaded; fertile, moist, but loose, acidic and shallow soil.

▬ USE: A plant which grows in rock gardens and rockeries as well as in plant containers. It is a good choice for moor beds, in combination with rhododendrons.

▬ CARE NOTE: The demanding perennial dislikes winter moisture. A cover against frost is advisable.

■ PROPAGATION: Sow fresh seeds immediately in the fall (they need cold to germinate) or divide bigger plants in winter. You can get shoots from spring to summer).

■ VARIETY TIP: 'Alba' has white flowers; 'Praecox' has dark blue flowers with appear approximately three weeks earlier than those of any other variety.

■ OTHER VARIETIES: The *G. septemfida* var. *lagodechiana* from the eastern Caucasus region flowers in violet-blue from July to September and is a nice complement to the Gentiana sino-ornata. It grows up to 12 inches tall and prefers limy soil.

Geranium x magnificum
Geranium

▬ FAMILY: *Geraniaceae*

▬ ORIGIN: Cultivation. A hybrid of *G. ibericum* and *G. platypetalum*, which is widespread from the Caucasus to Iran.

▬ GROWTH: 20 inches high; bushy, strong, spherical form.

▬ FOLIAGE AND FLOWERS: Rounded, lobed, dark green foliage turns, yellow-orange to sparkling red in the fall; spicy aroma. The dark violet, saucer-shaped flowers with dark veins sit in umbel-like flowers. Flowering period is from May to June.

▬ SITE: Sunny to semi-shaded; nutrient-rich, loose, moderately dry soil.

▬ USE: The vigorously growing perennial is suitable for large areas, perennial borders or as a foreground for or among woody plants. If planted in groups, a bare place can be greened immediately. The flowers last for quite a long time in a vase.

■ CARE NOTE: Cut back near the earth in winter.

■ PROPAGATION: The plants can be divided before or after flowering; sowing is possible in spring.

■ SPECIAL CHARACTERISTICS: This geranium has beautiful, decorative, spicy leaves and a striking fall color scheme even between its flowering periods.

■ OTHER VARIETIES: *G. x cantabrigiense,* 'Biokovo,' is a vigorously growing groundcover whose pink-white flowers appear from May to July (8 inches). *G. macrorhizum* grows in moist soil as well. Its softly pink, delicate spring flowers (10 inches). The name of the *G. sanguineum* refers to carmine flowers and to the blood-red fall color.

Geranium-Pratense-hybrid 'Johnson's Blue'
Geranium

Site:
☼ – ☼

Environment:
B F G W

Characteristics:

- FAMILY: *Geraniaceae*

- ORIGIN: CULTIVATION. This variety is native to Europe, but can be found in Siberia and Central Asia.

- GROWTH: 20 inches high; bushy, hemispherical.

- FOLIAGE AND FLOWERS: Fine, intensely green, deeply divided foliage. Violet-blue with light purple "eyes." Flowering period is from June to July-August.

- SITE: Sunny to semi-shaded; nutrient-rich, loose, limy, moderately moist soil.

- USE: This perennial fits into gardens with a rustic charm. It is perfect in front of and among trees and shrubs as well as on the banks of garden ponds and streams.

- CARE NOTE: Cut back substantially in winter.

■ PROPAGATION: The plants can be divided before or after flowering; sowing is possible in spring.

■ VARIETY TIP: 'Album' has white flowers, 'Mrs. Kendall Clarke' has light to violet-blue flowers, sometimes with white veins. The white flowers of 'Striatum' have striking violet striped. There are also varieties with double flowers.

■ OTHER VARIETIES: *G. renardii* is very suitable for the foreground of borders. It is bushy and compact and 12 inches high. Its deeply lobed, gray-green leaves attract attention together with tender, white flowers with violet veins. The variety 'Philippe Vapelle' has bigger, intensely blue-violet, veined flowers.

Glechoma hederacea 'Variegata'
Ground ivy

Site:

Environment:
G

Characteristics:

▬ FAMILY: *Lamiaceae*

▬ ORIGIN: The protected wild variety is native to European woods. The 'Variegata' is a form with varigated leaves.

▬ GROWTH: 6 inches high; spreads like a carpet through shoots, vigorously growing.

▬ FOLIAGE AND FLOWERS: Round, heart-shaped dark green leaves have large, rounded teeth on their white margins; spicy fragrance. The tiny, blue-violet flowers sit on erect whorls and release a pleasant aroma. Flowering period is from April to June.

▬ SITE: Semi-shaded to shady; nutrient-rich and fertile, moist soil.

▬ USE: This vigorously growing ground cover for shady areas of a garden overgrows walls or trellises as well. It is important to provide it with enough space. Astilbes and purple foxgloves are good planting partners. The variety 'Variegata' is also a very popular climber with ornamental foliage perfect for flower boxes and hanging pots or baskets.

■ CARE NOTE: If ground ivy grows too vigorously, it can be dug away and thus controlled. The soil should never be dry because the leaves brown quickly. This applies especially to plant containers where there is no water supply from deeper underground soil layers.

■ PROPAGATION: Separated shoots take root easily.

■ SPECIAL CHARACTERISTICS: Bees and bumblebees like its flowers. The perennial contains a slightly poisonous, bitter substance, which used to be used as a medicine.

■ VARIETY TIP: 'Rosea' enchants with its violet-pink flowers.

Gunnera tinctoria
Giant rhubarb

■ FAMILY: *Gunneraceae*

■ ORIGIN: The variety comes from Chile and is also well-known under its synonym, *G. chilensis*. It resembles the vegetable – *Rheum rhabarbarum*.

■ GROWTH: 80 inches high; wide bushy, grows robustly.

■ FOLIAGE AND FLOWERS: Huge (an average of 60 inches), round, deeply lobed, rough deep green leaves, with multi-toothed margins. The red-brown flowers sit in erect, conical spikes hidden under leaves. Flowering period is from July to August.

■ SITE: Sunny to semi-shaded and warm; nutrient-rich, fertile, moist to marshy soil.

■ USE: A striking solitary plant with ornamental leaves. Suitable for large gardens. It prefers growing on the banks of ponds and streams. Bamboo, hemp agrimony or plume poppy are ideal companions.

■ CARE NOTE: In the fall, the crown of the plant should be protected from frosts by mulching with dead leaves after cutting back. Late frosts are very dangerous for young shoots.

■ PROPAGATION: Divide in spring before the beginning of growth.

■ SPECIAL CHARACTERISTICS: The green leaves contrast dramatically with reddish stems. The flowers are followed by ball-shaped, red-tinged fruits.

■ OTHER VARIETIES: *G. manicata* from southern Brazil is as impressive as its relative.

Gypsophila paniculata
Baby's Breath

▬ FAMILY: *Caryophyllaceae*

▬ ORIGIN: The variety, also known as Chalk Plant, is widespread, from southern Europe to the Caucasus, Siberia and Central Asia.

▬ GROWTH: 40 inches high; loose, bushy and ball-shaped with tender shoots; richly branched, robust taproots.

▬ FOLIAGE AND FLOWERS: Narrowly lance-shaped, gray-green leaves. The small, double, white and pink flowers sit in loose panicles spread like a veil across the foliage. Flowering period is from July to September.

▬ SITE: Sunny, dry and warm – the perennial is sensitive to moisture; loose, deep, moderately dry – also limy – soil.

▬ USE: A perennial for beds and borders which presents a nice contrast to the colorful flowers of its neighboring plants. On that score, it is a good partner for ornamental perennials or roses. It is very popular as a cut or dried flower and is also impressive grown in a container.

■ CARE NOTE: If you do not regularly cut its branches for a vase, cutting back after the first flowering will ensure a second flowering.

■ PROPAGATION: Divide or sow in late winter or early spring. Shoots cut from April to May and cultivated at home, or in a greenhouse, take root well.

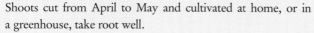

■ VARIETY TIP: The grandiflorous 'Bristol Fairy' has white double flowers (40 inches); 'Compacta Plena' has the same flowers, but is only 8 inches high and is suitable for rock gardens. 'Flamingo' (50 inches) enchants with pink double flowers.

■ OTHER VARIETIES: *G. repens* is 10 – 12 inches and has pink flowers.

Hakonechloa macra
Japanese forest grass

▬ FAMILY: *Poaceae*

▬ ORIGIN: This grass is native to the Japanese forest. The genus comprises only one variety.

▬ GROWTH: 12 inches high; lawn-like; slow growing.

▬ FOLIAGE AND FLOWERS: Oblong, lance-shaped, arching, fresh green leaves which turn bronze in the fall. Discrete spikes. Flowering period is from August to October.

▬ SITE: Sunny to semi-shaded, warm; fertile, moderately moist soil.

▬ USE: This lawn-like grass is ideal for borders. It fits well on the banks of ponds and streams or in the light shade of woody plants. Naturally, it grows in every Japanese garden. You can display it on your balcony or terrace as a hardy container plant.

▬ CARE NOTE: Winter protection is advisable for container plants. The grass does not tolerate any humidity.

■ PROPAGATION: The tufts can be divided in spring.

■ VARIETY TIP: 'Aureola' sets itself apart from the variety with its yellow striped leaves. The variety is suitable for semi-shaded areas in particular, which are brightened with its pale leaves.

■ OTHER VARIETIES: The Japanese blood grass *(Imperata cylindrica)* attracts attention until winter with its deep red stalks. The grass forms narrow, 20 inch high tufts and requires winter protection. There is also the variety 'Rubra' (syn. 'Red Baron').

Helenium-Hybrids
Sneezeweed

FAMILY: *Asteraceae*

ORIGIN: Cultivation. The wild varieties are often found in sunny California.

GROWTH: 30 – 60 inches high, based on the variety; upright, bushy.

FOLIAGE AND FLOWERS: Oblong, lance-shaped, dark green leaves. The tongue petals are arranged around a striking central disk; the color shades range from golden-yellow to red-brown and are sometimes also bicolored. Flowering period is from July to September.

SITE: Sunny, dry; nutrient-rich, fertile, moderately moist soil.

USE: A common central perennial for beds and borders; also suitable as a cut flower. Asters, fern-leaf yarrow, phlox, delphinium, eastern purple coneflower or high ornamental grasses complement it. Additionally, various varieties can be combined harmoniously with it.

■ CARE NOTE: Dividing every three or four years contributes to the plant's regeneration. The perennial should be cut back to the ground between fall and late winter.

■ PROPAGATION: Divide or cut ground shoots in spring.

■ SPECIAL CHARACTERISTICS: The flowers are continuously visited by bees and other kinds of the insects. If touched, the plant can irritate sensitive skin.

■ VARIETY TIP: The yellow flowers of 'Goldrausch' blaze from far away (55 inches). 'Moerheim Beauty' blooms very early and has plenty of coppery-red flowers (30 inches); the red 'Mahagoni' does not flower until August (35 inches). It distinguishes itself by yellow, pointed tongue petals.

Helianthemum-Hybrid 'Lawrenson's Pink'
Sunrose

▬ FAMILY: *Cistaceae*

▬ ORIGIN: Cultivation. The wild varieties originate in Europe, Asia Minor and North Africa.

▬ GROWTH: 8 inches high; bushy, low.

▬ FOLIAGE AND FLOWERS: Oblong, elliptical, dark green leaves with gray undersides. The saucer-shaped, solitary flowers form loose clusters; the flowers of 'Lawrenson's Pink' are pink with orange disks; other varieties are yellow, pink, red or white. Flowering period is from June to August.

▬ SITE: Sunny, warm and dry; loose, moderately dry, limy and shallow soil.

▬ USE: An ideal "sunny perennial" to border terraces and paths, strengthen open slopes, and to decorate rock gardens and gravel beds, containers and flower boxes. Other cushion perennials, sun-loving grasses and dwarf woody plants are perfect companions.

▬ CARE NOTE: If the plant loses its shape, it should be cut back after flowering. A protection from the bright winter sun is advisable.

▬ PROPAGATION: Cut green shoots take root well.

▬ SPECIAL CHARACTERISTICS: The sunrose is a semi-woody shrub, in which the crown of shoots lignifies. New herbaceous shoots develop from it every year.

▬ VARIETY TIP: The variety spectrum is big: 'Sterntaler' has sparkling yellow flowers, 'Gelbe Perle' has double, light yellow flowers. The double flowers of the 'Rubin' are ruby, 'Wisley White' blazes with white flowers.

Helleborus orientalis
Lenten rose

▬ FAMILY: *Ranunculaceae*

▬ ORIGIN: This variety comes from southeastern Europe and the Caucasus.

▬ GROWTH: 12 inches high; spreading in tufts through shoots.

▬ FOLIAGE AND FLOWERS: Hand-shaped, evergreen, dark green, glossy leaves with a leathery texture. The large, nodding, cup-shaped flowers sit on the end of the stems, which are greenish-white in this variety, but there are hybrid varieties in miscellaneous white, pink or red shades. Flowering period is from February to April.

▬ SITE: Semi-shaded to shady; nutrient-rich and fertile, moist, limy soil.

▬ USE: The original wild perennial is very impressive! It likes ferns, shade grasses or primroses. The small plant is also very popular as a potted or cut flower.

■ CARE NOTE: Robust, frost-tolerant hybrids can also grow in cool, shady places

■ PROPAGATION: Divide after flowering or sowing fresh seeds. The perennial also seeds abundantly on its own.

■ SPECIAL CHARACTERISTICS: Consumption can cause nausea and contact with the plant's juice can result in skin irritation.

■ VARIETY TIP: 'Spotted Hybrids' are a mixture of seedlings whose petals are spotted on the inside.

■ OTHER VARIETIES: The well-known, white Christmas rose *(H. niger)* begins flowering in December. It prefers dryer, even rocky, soil and is suitable for less sunny places. The purple flowers of *H. purpurascens* attract attention from February to April.

Hemerocallis-Hybrids
Daylily

Site:
☼ – ☼

Environment:
B W

Characteristics:
↷ 🗑 ✂

■ FAMILY: *Hemerocallidaceae*

■ ORIGIN: Cultivation. Many varieties come from the United States, the center for cultivation of Hemerocallis.

■ GROWTH: 15 – 40 inches high depending on the variety; wide tufted.

■ FOLIAGE AND FLOWERS: Slender, firm, arching, bright green foliage. Funnel-shaped flowers in yellow, orange, pink to red shades characterize the variety. The assortment offers large and small-flowered as well as fragrant varieties. Flowering period is from June to September.

■ SITE: Sunny, or semi-shaded; nutrient-rich, moderately moist to moist soil without humidity.

■ USE: A colored ornamental perennial for beds and borders, which likes growing near ponds as well. You should avoid planting them too tightly (25 – 35 inches) because they are very bushy. The low varieties are especially suitable for container planting; the tall ones are good as cut flowers.

▬ CARE NOTE: This perennial prefers growing in the same place for a long time. It expresses its gratitude for the occasional fertilization by flowering richly.

▬ PROPAGATION: Divide the rhizome after flowering, preferably before the beginning of spring.

▬ VARIETY TIP: It is difficult to choose from the huge assortment. The small-flowered, lemon-yellow 'Corky' is a well-known standard variety with a long flowering period. 'Stella de Oro' is only about 15 inches high. Its yellow-orange flowers have a tender scent.

▬ OTHER VARIETIES: In the evening, the slender, lemon-yellow flowers of the citron daylily *(H. citrina)* release a soft scent resembling that of lilies of the valley.

Heuchera americana 'Green Spice' Alumroot

▬ FAMILY: *Saxifragaceae*

▬ ORIGIN: Cultivation; the variety is also known as 'Eco Improved' and comes from North America.

▬ GROWTH: 25 inches high; foliage rosettes, bushy, forming thick flower cushions through shoots.

▬ FOLIAGE AND FLOWERS: Wide, heart-shaped, lobed leaves are winter green with grayish silver touches and purple-brown ribs. The small, cream-white flower bells sit in panicles at the end of the wiry flower shoots – they sail above the foliage like clouds. Flowering period is from May to June.

▬ SITE: Preferably semi-shaded, but also sunny; in nutrient-rich and fertile, well-drained, moderately moist soil.

▬ USE: Decorative foliage and flower perennial for semi-shaded beds and borders, as a foreground for woody plants, less sunny places in rock gardens or containers. Both leaves and flowers are suitable for flower arrangements.

■ CARE NOTE: The tufts should be regularly divided so as not to lose their growing and flowering intensity. Dry leaves and dead flowers should be removed in the fall.

■ PROPAGATION: Divide or sow in spring. The appearance of individual varieties usually varies in case of sowing.

■ OTHER VARIETIES: The evergreen *H. micrantha*, 'Palace Purple,' distinguishes itself with purple-brown leaves tinged with a bronze, metallic glimmer. Its reddish white bells appear from July to August. Plenty of hybrids have been developed as a result of crossbreeding of various varieties. One of them is the 'Red Sprangles' with scarlet panicles. 'Schneewittchen' has white flowers (both 20 inches high).

Hosta-Hybrid 'Hadspen Blue' Hosta

■ FAMILY: *Hostaceae*

■ ORIGIN: Cultivation. Most varieties of this genus are native to China, Japan and Korea.

■ GROWTH: 8 inches high; tufted, slow growing, flower shoots stand out erect from the foliage.

■ FOLIAGE AND FLOWERS: Heart-shaped, blue-gray, narrowly ribbed leaves. The light violet, trumpet-shaped flowers sit tightly packed in racemes. Flowering period is from June to July.

■ SITE: Semi-shaded; nutrient-rich and fertile, moist, but loose soil.

■ USE: The variety is used as a decorative, low ground cover for semi-shaded parts in a garden. In a container or flower box, it is a good choice for courtyards or northern balconies. Both leaves and flowers make every bouquet more attractive.

■ CARE NOTE: A mulch layer retains humidity in the soil. The leaves of the hostas are often infested by snails and slugs and it is necessary to check the plants regularly. The places where a hosta is planted should be marked so that the late sprouting perennials are not dug out by mistake.

■ PROPAGATION: Divide in early spring; varieties can also be sowed. If older rhizomes are very tough, use a knife.

■ OTHER VARIETIES: The spectrum of varieties is vast. 'Blue Danube' is the bluest hosta and is only 8 inches high; *H. sieboldiana* is about 25 inches high. The big, heart-shaped leaves of the variety 'Elegans' are blue-gray and soft lilac racemes appear in summer. 'Frances Williams' forms light violet flowers over gray-blue foliage with yellow margins.

Hosta 'Tardiflora'
Hosta

Site:
☼

Environment:
G W

Characteristics:
〜➔ ✂

▬ FAMILY: *Hostaceae*

▬ ORIGIN: Cultivation. The form is also well-known as *H. tardiflora*.

▬ GROWTH: 12 inches high; wide-tufted, forming thick groups over time.

▬ FOLIAGE AND FLOWERS: Round, lance-shaped leaves are glossy dark green on the top side and dull on the bottom side. The funnel-shaped, light blue-violet flowers sit at the end of slightly arching, purple-tinted stems. Flowering period is from August to September.

▬ SITE: Semi-shaded; in nutrient-rich and fertile, moist, but well-loosened soil.

▬ USE: An essential ornamental perennial for semi-shaded areas among, and in front of, woody plants. It also likes pond banks. In a container, it brightens less sunny balconies and makes terraces and courtyards more appealing.

■ CARE NOTE: These robust perennials spread willingly if they are allowed to grow without being disturbed. Otherwise, the same conditions apply as for the hosta 'Hadspen Blue.'

■ PROPAGATION: Divide in early spring; older, tough rhizomes can be cut if necessary.

■ VARIETY TIP: 'Halcyon' attracts attention with its gray-blue leaves and light violet flowers. The robust variety is resistant to snails and slugs.

■ OTHER VARIETIES: The 'Fortunei' group (formerly *H. x fortunei*) offers some yellow-green picotee varieties such as 'Fortunei Albopicta' or 'Goldstandard.' The green leaves of 'Francee' with their white margins are slender by comparison.

Iberis sempervirens
Candytuft

■ FAMILY: *Brassicaceae*

■ ORIGIN: The evergreen candytuft is widespread from southern Europe to Asia Minor.

■ GROWTH: 15 – 10 inches tall, depending on the variety; richly branched, forms thick flower cushions, woody or semi-woody shrub.

■ FOLIAGE AND FLOWERS: Lance-shaped, rough, evergreen, dark green foliage. Small, white, stellate flowers form thick corymbs. Flowering period is from April to June.

■ SITE: Sunny, warm and wind-protected; loose, dry to moderately moist, limy soil.

■ USE: This richly flowering cushion perennial is standard in every rock garden. It grows on dry walls and in shallow rocky areas. It can line flowerbeds and pathways or cover sharp edges of stairs. It can also be planted in containers and flower boxes. The white flowers form a harmonious contrast to its colorful neighbors – such as tulips or creeping phlox.

■■ CARE NOTE: Cutting back by approximately one-third after the first flowering promotes reflowering in the fall.

■■ PROPAGATION: Shoots cut from May to July take root easily. Or it can be sowed every spring.

■■ VARIETY TIP: 'Findel' (8 inches) and 'Schneeflocke' (10 inches) are popular, large-flowered and very hardy varieties. 'Zwergschneeflocke' is much smaller at 10 inches. 'Winterzauber' (8 inches) flowers early.

■■ OTHER VARIETIES: Perennial candytuft *(I. saxatilis)* forms very low, 8 inch high flower cushions.

Inula hookeri
Inula

Site:
☀ – ☀

Environment:
B F G

Characteristics:
🌱 ✂

■ FAMILY: *Asteraceae*

■ ORIGIN: The variety comes from the mountainous regions of the Himalayas.

■ GROWTH: 30 inches high; forming thick tufts.

■ FOLIAGE AND FLOWERS: Egg to lance-shaped, brilliant green leaves with serrated edges and a leathery texture. Slightly fragrant composite flowers with very long, narrow, yellow, tongue-like petals surround a center of brown-yellow tubular flowers. They appear alone or in clusters. Flowering period is from August to September.

■ SITE: Semi-shaded to sunny; deep, loose, moderately moist and nutrient-rich soil.

■ USE: With its "sunny" charisma, this wild perennial should have a place in every natural garden. It is an impressive background perennial for beds and borders due to its height.

▬ CARE NOTE: This Alant variety tolerates longer dry seasons without being damaged.

▬ PROPAGATION: Sow or divide in spring.

▬ SPECIAL CHARACTERISTICS: The sparkling, pleasantly scented flowers are magnets for bees and other insects. Unlike the following varieties, *I. hookeri* prefers semi-shaded places.

▬ OTHER VARIETIES: Swordleaf inula *(I. ensifolia)*, also known as dwarf swordleaf inula due to its compact size of 4 – 8 inches, likes full sun and is suitable for rock gardens and plant containers. Showy scabwort *(I. magnifica)* is an impressive central perennial in a flowerbed with a height of 70 inches.

Iris-Barbata-Hybrids
Bearded iris

▬ FAMILY: *Iridaceae*

▬ ORIGIN: Cultivation. The numerous forms of the bearded iris form one group in the iris genus.

▬ GROWTH: 6 – 50 inches high depending on the group; creeping rhizomes, flower shoots are simple or branched.

▬ FOLIAGE AND FLOWERS: Wide, sword-shaped, evergreen, gray-green foliage. The iris flower consists of three inner upright petals called standards and three outer petals known as falls; there is a line of white or colored hairs along the outer falls, due to which the iris is called "bearded." The assortment comprises almost all colors except red; partially fragrant. Flowering period is from April to July, based on the variety.

▬ SITE: Sunny and warm; in fertile and nutrient-rich, dry, loose, (slightly) limy soil.

▬ USE: Beautiful in beds and borders. Pure iris borders have a particular charm. Tall and medium varieties provide cut flowers; lower ones are suitable for rock gardens, flower boxes or bowls.

■ CARE NOTE: Fertilize with a fertilizer low in nitrogen shortly after planting directly before flowering. Don't mulch it because the rhizomes will rot. Bearded irises tolerate longer dry seasons; but in humid winters, you should expect rotting. The plants should be protected from frost.

■ PROPAGATION: Divide rhizomes after flowering and planting in such a way that the above ground parts lie open.

■ SPECIAL CHARACTERISTICS: All the plants are poisonous. The juice irritates the skin and consumption results in a heavy nausea.

■ VARIETY TIP: The choice is impressine, ranging from tall bearded irises (Iris Barbata-Elatior-group, 30 – 50 inches high), to the middle (Media-group, 15 – 30 inches) and low (Nana-group, 6 – 16 inches) varieties.

Iris reticulata
Dwarf iris

■ FAMILY: *Iridaceae*

■ ORIGIN: The netted iris, as the variety is also called, is native to Turkey, the Caucasus, Iraq and Iran.

■ GROWTH: 4 – 6 inches high; one or two leaves grow from one bulb.

■ FOLIAGE AND FLOWERS: Slender, sword-shaped, ribbed, 12 inch long leaves; gray green foliage. The upright standards are violet-blue, the outer falls have orange middle stripes. Soft scent. Flowering period is from February to March.

■ SITE: Sunny to semi-shaded, warm; sandy, loose, (slightly) limy soil.

■ USE: The dwarf iris belongs in a rock garden or rockery where it can grow among cushion plants. In early spring, it fills gaps in a flowerbed nicely. It is also suitable for flower bowls and pots.

■■■ CARE NOTE: A dry season should be enforced after flowering. The plants should be uncovered or dug out, cleaned and stored in a dry and well-ventilated place until the fall. Winter protection is necessary in cold regions.

■■■ PROPAGATION: In summer, bulbils, which emerge from the parent bulb under the net-like membrane, should be separated after the foliage has drawn in. These should be stored in a dry and well-ventilated place and planted about 2 – 3 inches deep in the fall.

■■■ SPECIAL CHARACTERISTICS: All plant parts are poisonous.

■■■ VARIETY TIP: 'Cantab' has pale blue flowers with yellow spots on the falls; 'J.S. Dijt' is purple with orange spots.

Kniphofia-Hybrids
Torch lily

■ FAMILY: *Asphodelaceae*

■ ORIGIN: Cultivation. These varieties come from Africa and Madagascar.

■ GROWTH: 25 – 40 inches high based on the variety; robust, upright flower shoots stand out from foliage tufts.

■ FOLIAGE AND FLOWERS: Narrow, linear, firm, evergreen, dark green foliage. The tubular flowers, mostly bicolored compact spikes, stand candle-like, while the yellow flowers blend into red. Flowering period is from June to September.

■ SITE: Sunny and warm, protected from wind and rain if possible; in nutrient-rich, moderately dry, well-drained soil.

■ USE: A sun lover for colorful borders. This perennial will grow in a container on a balcony and a terrace and is suitable as a cut flower.

■ CARE NOTE: The plant should be protected from humidity and severe (black) frosts in winter. For this purpose, the leaves should be bound together and the root area covered. The plant should be shortened by one third, but not until the spring.

■ PROPAGATION: Divide the robust rhizome in early spring or after flowering.

■ SPECIAL CHARACTERISTICS: The orange-red buds open in to yellow flowers. Since they open upwards, the flowers are bicolored for most varieties. The plant attracts bees and other insects.

■ VARIETY TIP: 'Royal Standard' has bicolored yellow and fire-red flowers (40 inches). The flower candles of 'Alcazar' are red; those of 'Sunningdale Yellow' are yellow (20 inches). The 'Bressingham' series appears in orange shades (30 inches).

Lamium maculatum 'Golden Anniversary'
Deadnettle

Site:

Environment:
G

Characteristics:

▬ FAMILY: *Lamiaceae*

▬ ORIGIN: Cultivation. The protected wild variety is indigenous from Europe to Siberia.

▬ GROWTH: 12 inches high; forms thick carpets through shoots, grows very rampant.

▬ FOLIAGE AND FLOWERS: Heart-shaped, crenate margin, softly haired; yellow-green picotee with white centers. Reddish-violet, whorl-like spikes. Flowering period is from May to June.

▬ SITE: Semi-shaded to shady; in nutrient-rich, fertile and moist soil.

▬ USE: Fast growing, luscious groundcover that grows in front of and among woody plants. It can also border less sunny terraces nicely. It is popular as a structural plant in flower boxes, hanging pots, baskets and containers as well.

■ CARE NOTE: Very rampant plants can be dug away or cut back. Otherwise, only dry leaves should be removed in the fall.

■ PROPAGATION: Divide in spring or in the fall, take cuttings from late spring to summer.

■ SPECIAL CHARACTERISTICS: The small flowers are very popular among bees and other insects.

■ VARIETY TIP: The green leaves of the 'Chequers' show a silvery central stripe. The variety has purple-pink flowers. 'Red Nancy' has almost white leaves and dark pink flowers; 'White Nancy' has white flowers over white leaves with green margins.

■ OTHER VARIETIES: Yellow Archangel (*L. galeobdolon*, syn. *Lamiastrum galeobdolon*) forms beautiful plants with silvery-white, marked foliage.

Lavandula angustifolia
Lavender

■ FAMILY: *Lamiaceae*

■ ORIGIN: The common lavender is native to the Mediterranean region.

■ GROWTH: 10 – 20 inches high depending on the variety; bushy branched, woody, semi-shrub.

■ FOLIAGE AND FLOWERS: Needle-like, aromatic, evergreen, gray-green foliage. The blue, violet or pink, two-lipped flowers sit in narrow spikes. Flowering period is from July to August.

■ SITE: Sunny and warm; nutrient-rich, sandy, loose, dry, preferably limy soil.

■ USE: The fragrant perennial releases a whiff of the Mediterranean whether in beds, borders, hedges, rock gardens or containers. It is appreciated as a companion for roses. Its flowers can be easily dried and used in small fragrant flower arrangements, such as potpourris or fragrant pillows.

CARE NOTE: Cut it back after flowering so that the plant remains bushy, but not too deep as it does not sprout well from the old wood. Protect it – especially container plants – from severe frosts.

PROPAGATION: Cut soft or half-ripe shoots in spring or after flowering; sow in early spring.

SPECIAL CHARACTERISTICS: The flowers attract bees and bumble-bees. Small bunches of lavender in a wardrobe should rout out moths.

VARIETY TIP: 'Hidcote Blue' with deep violet-blue flowers is very popular; 'Hidcote Pink' is its pink flowering counterpart. The light violet 'Dwarf Blue' is very compact with a height of 10 inches.

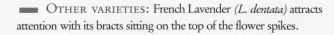

OTHER VARIETIES: French Lavender *(L. dentata)* attracts attention with its bracts sitting on the top of the flower spikes.

Lavatera olbia 'Rosea'
Tree mallow

Site:
☼

Characteristics:
B

Environment:

▬ FAMILY: *Malvaceae*

▬ ORIGIN: Cultivation. This variety can be found in southern Europe where it grows on rocky coastal stripes.

▬ GROWTH: Up to 80 inches high; an upright, bushy, branched, semi-shrub.

▬ FOLIAGE AND FLOWERS: Finger-like, three or five times lobed, soft, gray-felted, dull green foliage. Big, saucer-like, deep pink flowers sit at the end of shoots. Flowering period is from July to October.

▬ SITE: Sunny and warm, wind-protected; in nutrient-rich, well-drained and moderately moist soil.

▬ USE: As the plant flowers for a long time, it is suitable as a central plant for colorful beds and borders. At the same time, the blue shades of delphiniums and monkshoods contrast marvelously with the pink flowers of tree mallows; the flowers of tree mallows also last longer in a vase. The perennial is a decorative pot plant as well.

■ Care note: The beautiful flowers require adequate water and fertilization in summer. In winter, the plants must be covered, potted plants should be taken into the house and should spend the winter at 40 – 50°F. Oversize plants are thinned out and/or greatly cut back in spring or after flowering.

■ Propagation: Cuttings are taken from basal shoots in spring or in the fall.

■ Variety tip: The big, soft pink flowers of 'Barnsley' show a darker eye, turning almost white when withering (60 – 80 inches). They keep blooming tirelessly until the fall, often turning deep red after cutting back. 'Burgundy Wine' attracts attention with big wine flowers, while the flowers of 'Ice Cool' glow snow-white (both 30 – 40 inches).

■ Other varieties: The rosy tree mallow *(L. thuringiaca)* produces bright pink flowers for a long time.

Leucanthemum maximum
Shasta daisy

Site:
☼

Characteristics:
B

Environment:

■ FAMILY: *Asteraceae*

■ ORIGIN: This daisy variety originally comes from the Pyrenees and is also known as *Chrysanthemum maximum*. Many varieties are sold in stores.

■ GROWTH: 20 – 40 inches high depending on the variety; bushy, forming tufts through shoots.

■ FOLIAGE AND FLOWERS: Lance-shaped, fleshy; dark green, glossy foliage. Big, single or double heads with white tongue petals and a yellow central disk of tubular flowers. Flowering period is from July to September.

■ SITE: Sunny; in nutrient-rich, fertile, deep, moderately moist soil.

■ USE: If you want your beds and borders to have a natural character, plant this richly flowering perennial. It develops its full charm in small or larger groups. It forms colorful communities with delphiniums, lupins, bergamots, poppies or phlox; it is a beautiful companion for roses. Tall varieties are

especially popular cut flowers; shorter ones are suitable for borders. "Pot gardeners" can also enjoy this perennial.

■ CARE NOTE: Cutting back after the main flowering and additional fertilization will prompt a second flowering.

■ PROPAGATION: Divide in spring or after flowering.

■ VARIETY TIP: 'Beethoven' (30 inches) and 'Gruppenstolz' (20 inches) have single, white flowers. 'Christine Hagemann' and 'Wirral Supreme' (35 inches) have double ones.

■ OTHER VARIETIES: The white, daisy-like flowers of the oxeye daisy *(L. vulgare)* appear from late spring to early summer (25 inches).

Lewisia cotyledon
Bitter root

━ FAMILY: *Portulacaceae*

━ ORIGIN: The common bitter root is indigenous to the Rocky Mountain region of North America.

━ GROWTH: 8 inch high flower stalks stand out from flat rosettes of foliage.

━ FOLIAGE AND FLOWERS: Spoon-shaped, fleshy, ever-green foliage combines with star-like, pink and white striped flowers which form loose panicles. There are white, yellow, pink to red or striped varieties. Flowering period is from May to July.

━ SITE: Semi-shaded or sunny; not too nutrient-rich, loose, rocky, moderately moist soil, poor in lime.

━ USE: A perennial for collectors, which grows in less sunny places in rock gardens and rockeries and does well as a solitary or in groups. It grows on dry walls and rock gaps; balcony owners can also cultivate it in bowls and flower boxes. Hens and chicks, orpine and Dalmatian bellflower are its harmonious neighbors.

■ CARE NOTE: A gravel layer around the plant prevents rotting. Pot plants should not be watered too much and water standing in the rosette is to be avoided. The perennial should be protected from the bright winter sun.

■ PROPAGATION: Sow in spring, cut leaf shoots in summer. Hybrid varieties are not colorfast.

■ VARIETY TIP: The hybrid variety 'Sunset Strain' displays a brilliant interplay of red, orange or pink flowers.

Liatris spicata
Blazing star

Site:
☼

Environment:
B F

Environment:
 ✂

▬ FAMILY: *Asteraceae*

▬ ORIGIN: This species, rich in varieties, is indigenous to eastern North America.

▬ GROWTH: 30 inches high, upright, flower stalks with leaves stand out from a grass-like mop of leaves.

▬ FOLIAGE AND FLOWERS: Linear, grass-like leaves up to 15 inches long; stalk leaves are considerably smaller; foliage is intensely green. The small, lilac-pink heads sit on spadix-like spikes. Flowering period is from July to September.

▬ SITE: Sunny and warm; nutrient-rich, loose, not too moist soil.

▬ USE: A flowering perennial for sunny perennial borders, southern slopes and southern walls. It likes white bergamots, Italian asters, bellflowers or gray-foliage cushion perennials as its companions. It is also popular as a durable cut flower or a decorative container plant.

■ CARE NOTE: If you want to enjoy this perennial for a long time, fertilize it in spring and protect its tuberous roots from voles. It rots in heavy, moist soil during the winter.

■ PROPAGATION: Sow or divide in spring.

■ SPECIAL CHARACTERISTICS: The spikes flower downwards and are very attractive to butterflies.

■ VARIETY TIP: 'Kobold' has violet-pin flowers and, at 15 inches, is very compact. The bright violet 'Floristan Violett,' as well as the white 'Floristan Weiss,' are 30 – 35 inches high by comparison.

Ligularia dentata
Golden groundsel

▬ FAMILY: *Asteraceae*

▬ ORIGIN: This perennial, known also as orange ligularia bigleaf or ligularia leopard plant, comes from China and Japan.

▬ GROWTH: 40 – 60 inches high; bushy, forming tufts.

▬ FOLIAGE AND FLOWERS: Round, heart-shaped on the crown, crenate, ornamental leaves; foliage is green on the top side, purple underneath. Heads with narrow, yellow, tongue-shaped flowers with brown central disks float in corymbs over the foliage. Flowering period is from August to October.

▬ SITE: Semi-shaded, also sunny if the soil is damp; nutrient-rich, fertile, deep and moist soil.

▬ USE: The big, solitary perennial likes growing on the banks of pond, but it also finds its place in (large) perennial borders or in front of woody plants. Meadow sweet, daylilies, hemp agrimony, purple loosestrife, pendulous sedge or greater pond-sedge are good neighbors with similar requirements.

■ CARE NOTE: The otherwise modest perennial likes neither dryness nor heat. It is cut back to the ground in late winter.

■ PROPAGATION: Divide or sow in spring.

■ SPECIAL CHARACTERISTICS: The flowers offer bees plenty of nectar.

■ VARIETY TIP: 'Desdemona' and 'Othello' carry intensively orange-yellow flowers over purple foliage (40 inches). 'Moorblut' is only about 30 inches high and has light orange flowers.

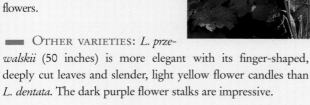

■ OTHER VARIETIES: *L. prze-walskii* (50 inches) is more elegant with its finger-shaped, deeply cut leaves and slender, light yellow flower candles than *L. dentata*. The dark purple flower stalks are impressive.

Lilium-Hybrids
Lily

Site:
☼ – ☼

Environment:
B F G

Characteristics:
↻ ▦ ✄ ⚠

▬ FAMILY: *Liliaceae*

▬ ORIGIN: Cultivation. These plants have developed from the crossbreeding of various wild varieties from North America, Europe and Asia. They are divided into nine classes; the Asian hybrids are common garden plants.

▬ GROWTH: 25 – 70 inches high based on the variety; bulbs are composed of fleshy leaf scales.

▬ FOLIAGE AND FLOWERS: Oblong, lance-shaped, dark green, glossy leaves. The lily flower consists of six identical petals arranged like a star with six stamens. It can be saucer-shaped, funnel-shaped, trumpet-shaped or turban-shaped and it sits on its own or in a group on upright, mostly non-branched flower shoots. The color spectrum comprises almost all shades excluding blue and black; many varieties are very fragrant. Flowering period depends on the variety and is from June to August or September.

▬ SITE: Sunny to semi-shaded, warm; root area should be shaded. It is best to protect the plant from wind and bad weather;

nutrient-rich, well-drained and looser, moderately moist, neutral to slightly acid soil.

▬ USE: Lily groups enhance perennial beds and borders and look very nice if accompanied by roses. Lilies can grow in the shade of trees only if the soil is not overgrown too much by roots. The lily is also popular as a cut flower and container plant.

▬ CARE NOTE: Lilies like staying in the same place for a long time. However, they should be fertilized with a preparation rich in potassium before and during sprouting. Excessive humidity should be avoided; the earth should be mulched. Dead flowers must be regularly removed; when the plant stops flowering, the bulbs should be divided and transplanted. The bulbs should not be exposed to the winter sun and should be protected from late frosts.

■ PROPAGATION: The method differs from variety to variety. You can separate bulbils or propagate scales from late summer to fall, but be careful – the bulbs dry out easily. The bulbs are preferably planted two to three times deeper than the height of the bulb in the fall or in spring. Some varieties can be sowed in spring, but you should be patient because seeds usually take several years to flower.

■ VARIETY TIP: The diversity of varieties is so extensive that choice can be difficult. 'Black Beauty' is an oriental hybrid with turban-shaped, fragrant flowers in deep black-red. 'Star Gazer,' a popular standard variety, has red flowers with white

margins. 'Journey's End' impresses with dark pink flowers with white margins.

'Bright Star' is a trumpet lily-hybrid with cream-white fragrant flowers. The petals are recurved on the top and the inner yellow central stripes look like a star.

'Connecticut King' with its intensively yellow, pendant flowers represents the Asian hybrids. 'Sterling Star' has cream-white flowers with dark spots. The orange-yellow flowers of 'Shuksan,' an American hybrid, are strikingly black-spotted.

■■■ OTHER VARIETIES: Besides the hybrids, there are also a number of related species. The Madonna lily or white lily *(L. candidum)* is one of them. It is approximately 40 inches high, has funnel-shaped, fragrant, pure white, flowers sitting in large numbers at the ends of the stalks. The Madonna lily blooms in July. The flower shoots of Henry's Lily *(L. henryi)* can grow up to 80 inches! It flowers from August to September and the flowers are orange-yellow with small brown spots. The variety 'Citrinum' has light lemon-yellow flowers. The Chinese Regal Lily *(L. regale)* justifies its name with its impressive, strongly fragrant flowers. Whites, trumpet-shaped flowers appear in July - they have yellow centers and brownish-red stripes on the outside.

Linum perenne
Blue flax

■ FAMILY: *Linaceae*

■ ORIGIN: The protected perennial flax is widespread from Europe to Siberia.

■ GROWTH: 20 inches high; upright, richly branched, forming tufts.

■ FOLIAGE AND FLOWERS: Linear, lance-shaped, bluish-green leaves. Funnel-shaped, pale blue flowers form thick corymbs. Flowering period is from May to July.

■ SITE: Sunny; in moderately nutrient-rich, sandy, loose, moderately dry and limy soil.

■ USE: An abundantly flowering, wild perennial for rock and heath gardens as well as natural perennial borders. It likes the company of low common yarrows, bellflowers, king's spear, dianthus, sunroses or festuca varieties. It looks nice as a low plant for borders as well as plant containers.

■ CARE NOTE: This dryness-tolerating perennial needs protection against winter wetness and frost.

■ PROPAGATION: Divide or sow in spring, cut soft or semi-ripe shoots from spring to summer. The perennial also seeds abundantly on its own.

■ SPECIAL CHARACTERISTICS: The flowers have mostly faded already by the time they began to bloom, but they appear in great numbers.

■ VARIETY TIP: 'Nanum Saphir' has blue flowers like the variety; 'Diamant' and 'Nanum Album' are white.

■ OTHER VARIETIES: Golden flax or goldflachs *(L. flavum)* owes its name to its big yellow flowers. It is about 12 inches high with blue-green foliage cushions. The Narbonne flax *(L. narbonense)* lifts sky-blue flowers over fine, lance-shaped leaves in summer.

Liriope muscari
Lily turf

■ FAMILY: *Convallariaceae*

■ ORIGIN: This perennial (syn. *Ophiopogon muscari*) comes from the forests of China, Japan and Taiwan.

■ GROWTH: 3 – 15 inches high; forms tufts.

■ FOLIAGE AND FLOWERS: Basal leaves are strap-shaped, grass-like, evergreen and dark green colored. Small deep violet flowers sit tightly packed on the ends of upright spikes. Flowering period is from August to November.

■ SITE: Semi-shaded to shady, warm, wind-protected; nutrient-rich, fertile, moist, but loose, acidic soil.

■ USE: Decorative, evergreen, wild perennial for shady areas of a garden. Rhododendrons, ferns, anemones and lily turfs (Ophiopogon) like the same environment. The lily turf is excellent as a potted plant.

■■■ CARE NOTE: The perennial can flower in a favorable place until frost. However, it must be kept away from the winter sun and temperatures below zero.

■■■ PROPAGATION: Either divide the plants in spring or sow the seeds in spring.

■■■ SPECIAL CHARACTERISTICS: The flowers are followed by abundant black berries.

■■■ VARIETY TIP: 'Curly Twist' has lilac racemes; 'Ingwersen' has violet ones. 'Lilac Beauty' attracts attention with its big flowers, while 'Golden Banded' has very impressive leaves with yellow margins.

Lobelia x speciosa
Lobelia

Site:
☼ – ☀

Environment:
B F

Characteristics:
🪴 ✂ 🔺

■ FAMILY: *Campanulaceae*

■ ORIGIN: Cultivation. The parent varieties come from North America.

■ GROWTH: 25 inches high; upright, scarcely branched.

■ FOLIAGE AND FLOWERS: Egg and lance-shaped leaves; dark, glossy green foliage. The lobelia flower consists of three bigger, lower and two smaller, upper petals that sit in great numbers on upright panicles. Flowering period is from June to August.

■ SITE: Sunny to semi-shaded; nutrient-rich, fertile, moist, but loose soil.

■ USE: Elegant flowering perennial for beds and borders; most beautiful in groups. It forms nice communities with beardtongue, bergenia, loosestrife, yellow monkey flower or alumroot. It is recommended as a potted plant and as a durable cut flower as well.

■ CARE NOTE: The frost-sensitive perennial must be covered well in winter or taken indoors.

■ PROPAGATION. Sowing indoors in January – February, planting out from mid-April. Often an annual plant.

■ SPECIAL CHARACTERISTICS: The panicles gradually start flowering upwards.

■ VARIETY TIP: The large-flowered 'Kompliment' series provides flowering beauty for weeks. Here it is possible to choose from among bright red, deep red and blue-violet shades (30 inches). The more compact 'Fan' Varieties (40 inches) are pink and red.

■ OTHER VARIETIES: The bright red cardinal flower *(L. cardinalis)* is suitable for the banks of ponds. The blue lobelia *(L. siphilitica)*, with its pure blue flowers, contrasts with the red color spectrum of the lobelias. Both of them are about 30 inches high.

Lupinus-Polyphyllus-Hybriden
Lupin

Site:
☼

Environment:
B

Characteristics:
🪣 ✂ !

▬ FAMILY: *Fabaceae*

▬ ORIGIN: Cultivation. The streamside lupin is descendent from the North American lupin *(L. polyphyllus)*.

▬ GROWTH: 30 – 50 inches high, depending on the variety; upright, bushy.

▬ FOLIAGE AND FLOWERS: Big, palmate leaves; egg-shaped to lance-shaped leaflets; dark green to bluish green foliage. Numerous pea-like flowers sit in long, candle-like racemes. The color spectrum is extensive and comprises white, pink, red and yellow to blue shades. Flowering period is from May to July, reflowering in September.

▬ SITE: Sunny and warm; in moderately nutrient-rich, light, deep, not too wet, slightly acidic soil.

▬ USE: The imposing bed perennial is common rural gardens. It is most beautiful in colorful groups. Smaller varieties also grow in containers; the flower candles look nice in vases.

■ CARE NOTE: Cutting back after flowering keeps the plant in a good condition and ensures a second flowering. However, the freshly sprouting leaves should be spared.

■ PROPAGATION: Sow in spring or cut non-flowering side shoots. The seeds should soak in water for 24 hours before being sowed.

■ SPECIAL CHARACTERISTICS: Root nodules collect nitrogen, thus increasing the nitrogen content in the soil. The seeds contain a poisonous alkaloid.

■ VARIETY TIP: The 'Russel' hybrids occur in various color shades with romantic names like 'Burgfräulein' (cream-white) or 'Edelknaben' (carmine). Since they are propagated through seeding, their color shades can vary slightly. The 'Gartenzwerg' and 'Gallery' color mixtures are compacter with their height of 25 inches.

Luzula nivea
Snowy woodrush

Site:

Environment:
G

Characteristics:

■ FAMILY: *Juncaceae*

■ ORIGIN: This grass is indigenous to southern Europe.

■ GROWTH: 8 inches high (with flowers of 15 inches); grassy tufts.

■ FOLIAGE AND FLOWERS: Slender, linear, grass-like evergreen leaves, fringed with silvery hairs; brilliantly green foliage. Small, whitish, solitary flowers float like snowflakes above foliate tufts. Flowering period is from June to July.

■ SITE: Preferably semi-shaded, also sunny; fertile, loose, moderately moist and acid soil.

■ USE: The tender grass likes growing in the shade of trees and shrubs, and is especially decorative in groups. It is suitable for semi-shaded borders; the dried flowers are a nice addition to flower arrangements.

■ CARE NOTE: Do not plant it in dark shade. Cut it back in late winter or in early spring.

■ PROPAGATION: The plants should be divided as soon as they start growing in spring. Sowing is also possible.

■ VARIETY TIP: 'Schneehäschen' is especially striking with its silvery-white leaves and white flowers.

■ OTHER VARIETIES: Hairy woodrush *(L. pilosa)* has brownish-green leaves and brownish spikes. The great wood-rush 'Marginata' *(L. sylvatica)*, attracts attention with its yellow-edged leaves and silvery spikes.

Lysimachia punctata
Garden loosestrife

Site:

Environment:
G B W F

Characteristics:

■ FAMILY: *Primulaceae*

■ ORIGIN: The variegated yellow loosestrife is widespread from the eastern Mediterranean region into the north of Italy and Asia Minor.

■ GROWTH: 30 inches high; upright, sparsely branched stalks; it spreads through shoots, making thick tufts.

■ FOLIAGE AND FLOWERS: Lance-shaped to elliptical whorls of bright green foliage. The small, bright yellow, star-like flowers are borne in the axils of the leaves at the ends of vertical stems. Flowering period is from June to August.

■ SITE: Semi-shaded to shady, also sunny with high soil humidity; nutrient-rich, loamy and moist soil.

■ USE: This perennial likes the shady vicinity of woody plants. It also does well in less sunny borders or in the shade of walls, as well as on banks of ponds and streams. The flowers fit in with summer flower arrangements.

CARE NOTE: This plant forms thick vegetation in no time!

PROPAGATION: Divide tufts in spring or fall. This is also wise when the plant expands too much.

VARIETY TIP: 'Alexander' distinguishes itself by its white leaves. 'Hometown Hero' has deep yellow flowers in long racemes.

OTHER VARIETIES: The yellow flowering moneywort (2 inches high) *(L. nummularia)* provides a good groundcover for moist, shady sites. The variety 'Aurea' attracts attention with its golden-yellow foliage. The purple gooseneck loosestrife *(L. atropurpurea)* impresses with its dark purple spikes.

Lythrum salicaria
Purple loosestrife

- FAMILY: *Lythraceae*

- ORIGIN: This loosestrife variety can be found across Europe, Asia and North Africa.

- GROWTH: 40 inches high; upright, bushy, forms tufts.

- FOLIAGE AND FLOWERS: Oval to narrowly lance-shaped leaves, arranged opposite each other on a square stalk; fresh green, often coppery-red in the fall. Many funnel-shaped, purple flowers sit on flower candles. Flowering period is July to September.

- SITE: Sunny to semi-shaded; nutrient-rich, loamy, moist or damp soil.

- USE: A richly flowering wild perennial for the banks of ponds, permanent swamps or moist meadows. Some varieties tolerate dryness and also grow in flowerbeds. Potential neighbors that can withstand the competition are astilbes, sagebrush, loosestrife, yellow monkey flower or Siberian iris. The flowers are durable when cut and good for drying.

■ CARE NOTE: Since the stalk lignifies, the plant can be cut back before winter.

■ PROPAGATION: Sow or divide in spring. Shoots of non-flowering side shoots also take root well.

■ SPECIAL CHARACTERISTICS: The long-flowering plant is extremely attractive to bees, butterflies and other kinds of insects. An extract from the roots can be applied as a styptic preparation.

■ VARIETY TIP: 'Blush' has salmon-pink flowers (30 inches), 'Feuerkerze' and 'Rosensäule' show deep pink flowers (50 inches). The dark red 'Zigeunerblut' is 50 inches high; the carmine 'Robert' is much smaller and more compact with a height of 25 inches.

■ OTHER VARIETIES: The pink-red wand loosestrife (*L. virgatum*) is only 25 inches high and has a more delicate appearance.

Macleaya cordata
Plume poppy

■ FAMILY: *Papaveraceae*

■ ORIGIN: The variety comes from China, Japan and Taiwan.

■ GROWTH: 80 inches high; upright, tufted, grows rampantly through offshoots.

■ FOLIAGE AND FLOWERS: Large, rounded to heart-shaped leaves which are blue-green on the top, white, downy haired underneath and often yellow in the fall. The small, beige to bronze flowers form big, feathery panicles. Flowering period is from July to August.

■ SITE: Sunny, also semi-shaded and warm; nutrient-rich, light, dry to moderately moist soil.

■ USE: This decorative wild perennial is impressive on its own or in groups in front of a neutral background such as woody plants, hedges, walls or along fences. Its height can be a means of guarding the privacy of your garden against unwelcome glances. High sunflowers are suitable companions.

■ CARE NOTE: The plant needs cutting back in late fall or late winter. But young shoots are endangered by late frosts. Planted in a container, it cannot grow abundantly.

■ PROPAGATION: Divide in spring, cut of rhizome shoots during the winter rest period.

■ SPECIAL CHARACTERISTICS: The stalks and leaves contain a brownish milky juice, which can irritate the skin.

■ VARIETY TIP: 'Korallenfeder' is distinctive with its coppery-red panicles and cinnamon-colored leaves.

■ OTHER VARIETIES: *M. microcarpa*, with its yellowish-brown flowers and blue-green leaves, is especially suitable for banks of ponds, lakes or streams.

Meconopsis grandis
Himalayan blue poppy

■ FAMILY *Papaveraceae*

■ ORIGIN: Nepal, Sikkim and Tibet.

■ GROWTH: 50 inches high; upright, forming tufts, with robust, hairy, red-brown flower shoots.

■ FOLIAGE AND FLOWERS: Oblong-shaped leaves with serrated margins located in basal rosettes and on the shoots; dark green foliage with red-brown hair. The flat, saucer-shaped, nodding flowers are sky-blue with a silky gloss. The yellow stamens contrast with the petals. The flowers sit individually on the axils of the leaves. Flowering period is from June to July.

■ SITE: Semi-shaded, cool, wind-protected; nutrient-rich, fertile, moist, loose, slightly acidic soil.

■ USE: This perennial prefers shady, woody areas with humid air. It complements rhododendron groups, ferns and grasses excellently.

CARE NOTE: Water it abundantly in summer; otherwise it will die soon after flowering. Remove seeds in order to prolong the flowering and lifespan of the plant. Late frosts can be dangerous for young plants.

PROPAGATION: This short-lived perennial should be divided after flowering. Ripe seeds should be sowed directly or stored until spring.

SPECIAL CHARACTERISTICS: The sky-blue flowers present an extraordinary picture.

OTHER VARIETIES: The flowers of the blue poppy *(M. betonicifolia)* are also blue, but smaller. The variety 'Alba' has white flowers. The Welch poppy *(M. cambrica)* with yellow flowers is well-known. This short-lived, robust perennial grows in limy soil.

Melica nutans
Nodding melick

Site:
☼ – ☼

Environment:
F S G B

Characteristics:
⟿ ↝ ▦ ✂

■ FAMILY: *Poaceae*

■ ORIGIN: This protected grass grows in deciduous woods from Europe to the Caucasus and Central Asia.

■ GROWTH: 15 – 25 inches high; forming loose tufts, spreading through offshoots into the form of a lawn.

■ FOLIAGE AND FLOWERS: Slender, linear, rolled, 8 inch leaves; fresh green, glossy foliage. Purple-brown, oblong spikes on elegantly hanging flower shoots. Flowering period is from May to June.

■ SITE: Sunny to semi-shaded; moderately nutrient-rich, moist, but loose and stony soil.

■ USE: Since it forms thick vegetation, the grass can be used for greening larger areas. It is best to plant it in bigger groups. It grows in a rock garden as well as in the changing shade of woody plants, mixed perennial borders or in a container. The spikes are easily dried and added to bouquets and flower arrangements.

▬ CARE NOTE: It should be protected from excessive wetness.

▬ PROPAGATION: Divide or sow in spring.

▬ OTHER VARIETIES: Purple Siberian melick 'Atropurpurea' *(M. altissima)* forms large, purple-brown panicles from May to June and grows in the sun as well as in half-shade. Silky spike melick *(M. ciliata)* prefers dry soil. Whitish-yellow spikes appear over the gray-green foliage in summer. The variety 'Erecta' attracts attention with its thick, white spadixes. The leaves of wood melick *(M. uniflora)* are striped cream-white.

Mimulus luteus
Yellow monkey flower

■ FAMILY: *Scrophulariaceae*

■ ORIGIN: The plant, also known as 'monkey musk,' comes from Chile.

■ GROWTH: 8 to 12 inches high; upright to creeping, roots grow on stalks.

■ FOLIAGE AND FLOWERS: Oblong-elliptic, crenate leaves; fresh green foliage. There are also hybrids with red spotted flowers as well as the lemon-yellow variety. The flowers mostly sit in racemes. Flowering period is from June to September.

■ SITE: Sunny to semi-shaded; in nutrient-rich, fertile, moist or wet soil.

■ USE: This richly and long-time flowering yellow monkey flower prefers the moist banks of ponds, lakes or streams and even the swamp area of a garden pond (to the depth of 4 inches). It spreads easily by dropping seeds. Forget-me-nots and globeflowers are suitable companions.

■ CARE NOTE: Protection from black frost is recommended.

■ PROPAGATION: Sow or divide from late winter to early spring; cut off shoots in early summer.

■ VARIETY TIP: The yellow flowers of 'Tigrinus Grandiflorus' are strikingly red spotted.

■ OTHER VARIETIES: Lavender musk, *M. ringens*, (30 inches high) likes growing on banks as well. It attracts attention with its blue-violet flowers. The big, scarlet, tubular flowers of *M. cardinalis* (20 – 30 inches high) emerge in great numbers from June to September. This colorful, long flowering plant also grows in the moderately dry soil of perennial borders, in rock gardens or in plant containers.

Miscanthus sinensis
Miscanthus

▬ FAMILY: *Poaceae*

▬ ORIGIN: The variety is indigenous to China.

▬ GROWTH: 40 – 80 inches high, depending on the variety; tufted; the flowers stand out from the foliage.

▬ FOLIAGE AND FLOWERS: Linear, reed-like, mostly arching leaves; foliage is green, but many varieties change color in the fall. Feathery panicles in various color combinations. Flowering period is from July to October.

▬ SITE: Sunny; nutrient-rich, loamy, moderately moist soil.

▬ USE: Decorative solitary perennial for the background of perennial borders, an eye catcher in lawns or on the banks of ponds. A necessity for a pure grass garden and also a means of ensuring your privacy against unwanted glances. Shorter varieties are suitable for plant containers; the leaves as well as the dried flowers can be used in flower arrangements.

■ CARE NOTE: Grasses covered with hoarfrost are decorative in winter too, so the plant should not be cut back until spring. The foliage should be bound together in winter to protect against wetness and frost.

■ PROPAGATION: Divide in spring at the beginning of growth.

■ VARIETY TIP: 'Kleine Fontäne' distinguishes itself with slender leaves and silvery-pink panicles (70 inches). Cross stripes on the green, arching leaves of 'Strictus' are striking. The variety grows up to 60 inches high, but the flowers appear only in warm summers. 'Malepartus' has feathery, red-brown panicles and grows up to 80 inches high. The foliage turns strikingly red-brown in the fall. 'Silberfeder' is a fall-flowering variety with silvery spikes and slender leaves. 'Yakushima Dwarf, with silvery spikes, is only 40 inches high and is suitable for plant containers.

Molinia caerulea 'Moorhexe'
Purple moorgrass

■ FAMILY: *Poaceae*

■ ORIGIN: Cultivation. The protected variety - purple moorgrass - is widespread in moor areas of Europe and West Asia.

■ GROWTH: 8 inches high, with flowers 30 inches high; cluster-like, thick tufts, with upright flower stalks standing radialy from the foliage.

■ FOLIAGE AND FLOWERS: Slender, linear, golden-yellow foliage in the fall. Dark purple spikes in loose panicles. Flowering period is from August to October.

■ SITE: Sunny to semi-shaded; moderately nutrient-rich, fertile, moist, loose, neutral to acidic soil.

■ USE: The name indicates that this delicate grass is especially suitable for heath and moor gardens. It can also be integrated in front of and among woody plants or in mixed borders. It stands out impressively from a cover of cushion grasses such as festuca; it is also very decorative in mixed plant containers. Leaves and dried flowers are often added to flower arrangements.

▬ CARE NOTE: Do not cut it back until spring because moorgrass covered with hoarfrost in winter is beautiful.

▬ PROPAGATION: Sow or divide in spring.

▬ VARIETY TIP: 'Heidebraut' rises to a height of 60 inches. 'Moorflamme'

is an eye catcher in a garden with its reddish, fall color. 'Variegata' is impressive with green and cream-white striped leaves. The foliage mops are only 12 inches high; the brownish flowers rise to a height of 20 inches.

Monarda-Hybrid 'Squaw'
Bergamot

Site:
☼ – ☀

Environment:
B F G

Characteristics:

- **FAMILY:** *Lamiaceae*

- **ORIGIN:** Cultivation. The parent varieties come from North America.

- **GROWTH:** 40 inches high; upright, bushy, forming thick vegetation through offshoots.

- **FOLIAGE AND FLOWERS:** Egg to lance-shaped, fragrant, green leaves, with distinct ribbing. Bright scarlet, two-lipped flowers sit in several layered whorls. Flowering period is from June to August.

- **SITE:** Sunny to semi-shaded, warm; nutrient-rich, fertile, moderately moist, loose soil.

- **USE:** A robust, long flowering plant for colorful beds and semi-shaded, woody plant borders. Grasses, white astilbes, snakeroots, baby's breath, yellow daylilies, goldenrod and eastern purple coneflower are its favorite companions. Bergamot also makes a durable cut flower or potted plant.

■ CARE NOTE: The soil should be allowed to dry out in summer and the plant should be protected from excessive wetness in winter. It should be cut back greatly in the late fall or in late winter.

■ PROPAGATION: Sow or divide in spring; upper or basal shoots should be cut from late spring to summer.

■ SPECIAL CHARACTER-ISTICS: A popular plant for butterflies. The fragrant leaves of *M. didyma* are still used for flavoring tea. The Indians used it as a treatment for colds in the past.

■ VARIETY TIP: The well-known 'Beauty of Cobham' forms lilac-pink flowers over purple-green foliage; 'Cambridge Scarlet' has scarlet flowers. The bright pink 'Marshall's Delight' and the lilac 'Mohawk' are new on the market. The flowers of 'Schneewittchen' are bright white.

Myosotis sylvatica
Forget-me-not

Site:
☼ – ☼

Environment:
B F G

Characteristics:
🧺 ✂ 🏵

FAMILY: *Boraginaceae*

ORIGIN: The protected variety is native to Europe and is widespread in Asia. Besides the wild form, there are a great number of varieties.

GROWTH: 4 – 12 inches high depending on type; basal foliage rosettes; bushy, stender, upright.

FOLIAGE AND FLOWERS: Oblong, downy leaves; dark green foliage. Plenty of small, blue, pink or white solitary flowers (depending on the variety) cover the foliage almost completely. Flowering period is from April to June.

SITE: Sunny to semi-shaded, cool; nutrient-rich, fertile, loamy and loose soil.

USE: A colorful spring flower for beds and edges, plant pots and small flower arrangements. It can be combined with bulb flowers of its season and its natural charm is also suitable for wild gardens.

▬ CARE NOTE: Cutting back after flowering prevents the plant from dropping seeds naturally. It will survive long, cold winters with protection.

▬ PROPAGATION: Usually a biannual plant. If seeds are not sowed directly at the appropriate site in the summer, they can be sowed indoors in spring and planted out in summer or the following spring.

▬ VARIETY TIP: The compact 'Blaue Kugel' (6 inches) fits well in bowls and flower boxes; 'Blauer Strauss' (12 inches) is an ideal cut flower. 'Dunkelblauer Turm' (10 inches) is suitable for flowerbeds as well as for flower arrangements. The variety 'Rosylva' has pink flowers (8 inches).

▬ OTHER VARIETIES: True forget-me-nots *(M. palustris)* prefer the banks of ponds, lakes or streams. Their dark blue flowers bloom profusely from May to September. The variety 'Thüringen' has light blue flowers.

Nepeta racemosa 'Superba'
Catmint

▬ FAMILY: *Lamiaceae*

▬ ORIGIN: The wild variety (syn. *N. x faassenii, N. mussinii*) is found in the Caucasus and Iran.

▬ GROWTH: 10 inches high; bushy, tufted.

▬ FOLIAGE AND FLOWERS: Narrow, egg-shaped, fragrant leaves and gray-green foliage. The two-lipped, deep lavender-blue flowers are arranged in whorls on the stalk. Flowering period is from May to September.

▬ SITE: Sunny, warm; loose, dry soil.

▬ USE: A flowering perennial for sunny beds and slopes, rock and steppe gardens or exposed roof gardens. It can be used for bordering paths and terraces, in plant pots or as a companion for roses. Varieties combine very well.

▬ CARE NOTE: Cutting back after the first flowering, and an additional fertilization, will prompt another bloom. The perennial should be cut back to the ground in late fall or in late winter.

■■■ PROPAGATION:
Divide in spring. Cut
soft or half-ripe shoots
in summer and fall.

■■■ SPECIAL CHAR-
ACTERISTICS: The scent
attracts cats, who like
rolling around in the plant
or eating it. The flowers
are popular with bees and
butterflies.

■■■ VARIETY TIP: 'Grog' distinguishes itself by dark lilac-
blue flowers, strikingly lilac-red calyces and a lemon scent. The
white 'Snowflake' is shorter at 10 inches, but it grows exten-
sively.

■■■ OTHER VARIETIES: *N. x faassenii,* 'Six Hills Giant,' is
a popular variety with lavender-blue flowers (20 inches). The
pink flowers of *N. grandiflora,* 'Dawn to Dusk,' the giant catmint, rise to the height of 25 inches.

Nymphaea-Hybrids
Water lily

Site:
☼

Environment:
W

Characteristics:
🌱 ✂ 🔥

▬ FAMILY: *Nymphaeaceae*

▬ ORIGIN: Cultivation. Wild varieties are widespread all over the world.

▬ GROWTH: The leaves float on the water's surface, the flowers cover the leaves; roots in the earth.

▬ FOLIAGE AND FLOWERS: Round leaves with diameters up to 12 inches. Green or red-brown foliage. Saucer, cup or star-shaped; blossoms in red, pink, yellow or white, depending on the variety. Flowering period is from June to November.

▬ SITE: Sunny; loamy soil, warm water poor in lime, for depths of 12 – 30, depending on the variety.

▬ USE: A plant with floating leaves for large and small garden ponds and water containers. If put in the sun, the cut flowers last in a vase for approximately 30 minutes before closing.

■ CARE NOTE: Exotic, non-hardy varieties spend the winter in a house (e.g. in a container with moist sand). All the others can stay outside in ponds that are deeper than 20 inches. Plants growing in baskets should be fertilized regularly and replanted every two or three years.

■ PROPAGATION: Divide, separate seedlings, cut rhizome shoots or sow in spring.

■ VARIETY TIP: The variety is unlimited. However, you must take into consideration the depth and winter hardiness as well as the flower color when you choose a variety. 'Attraction' with pink flowers and yellow centers, the red 'Escarboucle,' 'Hermine' with white, stellate flowers, the pink-red 'James Brydon,' 'Marliacea Albida' with white, fragrant flowers or the pale yellow 'Marliacea Chromatella' are standard robust varieties. Dwarf water lilies are suitable for shallow water.

Oenothera fruticosa
Evening primrose

Site:
☼

Environment:
B F S

Characteristics:
🏺 � ✂

▬ FAMILY: *Onagraceae*

▬ ORIGIN: The variety, also well-known as *O. tetragona*, comes from North America.

▬ GROWTH: 25 inches high; upright, forms loose tufts.

▬ FOLIAGE AND FLOWERS: Lance-shaped; dark green stained with bronze. Big, cup-shaped flowers glow warm golden-yellow. Flowering period is from June to August.

▬ SITE: Sunny and warm; nutrient-rich, deep, dry to moderately moist and loose soil.

▬ USE: Multi-purpose, flowering perennial suitable for beds and borders, natural perennial meadows, rock gardens, plant boxes and as a cut flower. The glaring flower color is especially conspicuous in groups. Asters, lychnises, common gypsyweeds, high bellflowers, catmints and sage varieties make good neighbors.

■ CARE NOTE: A firm cutting in the fall, or in late winter at the latest, ensures an early flowering of multi-annual crops.

■ PROPAGATION: Sow in spring or cut soft shoots in early summer. The modern hybrid varieties are mostly cultivated only for one or two years.

■ SPECIAL CHARACTERISTICS: The flowers do not open until the evening, when they attract owlet moths with their sweet scent.

■ VARIETY TIP: The yellow 'Fry-verkeri' has striking red buds (15 inches). 'Hohes Licht' has light yellow flowers; 'Sonnenwende' has golden-yellow flowers and reddish foliage (both 25 inches).

■ OTHER VARIETIES: The yellow Missouri evening-primrose *(O. macrocarpa)* grows 8 inches high and is ideal for rock gardens and borders. *O. speciosa* offers varieties with pink flowers.

Onoclea sensibilis
Bead fern

■ FAMILY: *Woodsiaceae*

■ ORIGIN: The genus consists only of one species native to most areas of North America and East Asia.

■ GROWTH: 15 – 20 inches high; forms thick fern tufts and spreads through creeping rhizomes.

■ FOLIAGE: The sterile fronds are broad, deeply pinnate, light green, yellow-brown in the fall. Slender, upright, spore-bearing fronds sprout in summer. The feathery spores are arranged like a pearl necklace.

■ SITE: Semi-shaded to shady; on the banks of ponds; also in sunny, wind protected, humid places and in nutrient-rich, fertile, moist to wet, preferably acid soil.

■ USE: This fern is a good choice for larger gardens because it spreads well. It grows in the shade of woody plants and walls as well as on banks of ponds and streams. It forms nice plant groups in darker corners together with other shade-tolerating perennials such as goatbeard, snakeroot, hosta or

royal fern. Dried spore-bearing fronds can be used in flower arrangements.

■ CARE NOTE: It is recommended to enrich the soil with manure, foliage soil and wood pieces before planting. Ferns prefer growing in the same place for many years.

■ PROPAGATION: Divide in spring.

■ SPECIAL CHARACTERISTICS: While the infertile fronds freeze, the fertile fronds survive the winter.

■ OTHER VARIETIES: The elegant maidenhair fern *(Adiantum pedatum)* likes the same conditions as the bead fern. Black-stemmed, green fronds are striking, as is the coppery yellow fall color.

Osmunda regalis
Royal fern

 FAMILY: *Osmundaceae*

 ORIGIN: The variety, also known as the flowering fern, originally comes from Canada and North America. It grows in nature in moorland and wooded areas and is now protected.

 GROWTH: 30 – 50 inches high; upright, forming loose tufts.

 FOLIAGE: Broadly oblong, double-pinnate, up to 80 inches long, pale green sterile fronds. Brown spore capsules appear on the inside of the fronds.

 SITE: Semi-shaded to shady; nutrient-rich, fertile, acid and moderately moist soil.

 USE: The ornamental fern likes growing in moist areas near ponds or streams or in the shade of woody plants. The shape of the solitary plant is very impressive. Astilbes, monks-hoods, barrenworts and primroses are good neighbors.

 CARE NOTE: As with many ferns, the royal fern prefers growing in the same place for many years without being dis-

turbed. We recommend that you enrich the soil with manure, foliage soil and wood pieces before planting.

■ PROPAGATION: Sow ripe seeds immediately in late spring because they lose their ability to sprout quickly. Large groups can be divided in spring.

■ SPECIAL CHARACTERISTICS: The royal fern is one of the biggest ferns in the world.

■ VARIETY TIP: 'Gracilis' is compact with its height of 25 – 30 inches. The dwarf royal fern turns strikingly brown in the fall. The variety 'Purpurascens,' also known as purple-stemmed royal fern, makes a nice picture with its coppery red fronds (50 inches).

Oxalis species
Common sorrel

■ FAMILY: *Oxalidaceae*

■ ORIGIN: The genus comprises approximately 500 species native to South Africa and South America. Some varieties grow in cooler woodland regions from Europe to Central Asia.

■ GROWTH: 4 – 6 inches high; cushion-like, spreading through bulbs, rhizomes or tubers.

■ FOLIAGE AND FLOWERS: Digitate, clover-like leaves; pale to dark green based on the variety, silvery, glossy or sometimes reddish-brown foliage. Funnel to saucer-shaped, often pink or yellow (*O. lobata*) flowers. Flowering period is from April to September.

■ SITE: Varieties from warm regions need moderately nutrient-rich, loose soil and sun. Varieties from woodland regions grow in the shade in nutrient-rich, moist, fertile and preferably acidic soil.

■■ USE: The sun-loving varieties such as *O. adenophylla* or *O. bowiei* enrich any rock garden and also grow down walls. Woodland varieties such as *O. acetosella* form flowering carpets under woody plants. You can plant the common sorrel in bowls and flower boxes on your balcony and terrace; it grows as a potted plant in a cold room as well.

■■ CARE NOTE: Varieties needing warmth, such *O. bowiei*, need a light winter protection in cold regions.

■■ PROPAGATION: Sow in early spring. Separate small tubers or bulbils and/or divide rhizomes.

■■ SPECIAL CHARACTERISTICS: Leaves and flowers usually open only when the sun is shining. They stay closed at night and in rainy weather.

Paeonia-Lactiflora-Hybriden
Peony

Site:
☼

Environment:
B

Characteristics:
↻ ✂ !

■ FAMILY: *Paeoniaceae*

■ ORIGIN: The common garden peony or Chinese peony (syn. *P. albiflora, P. sinensis*) comes from China, Tibet and Siberia.

■ GROWTH: 25 – 40 inches high; broadly fruticose, tufted.

■ FOLIAGE AND FLOWERS: Pinnate or firm, dark green blue or gray-green foliage. The most common variety has single, white to pink flowers and is fragrant, but other varieties have single, saucer-shaped to fully double, ball-shaped, partially fragrant flowers in white, yellow, pink and red shades. Flowering period is from May to June.

■ SITE: Sunny and warm; nutrient-rich, loamy, deep, loose, moderately moist and slightly acidic soil.

■ USE: A traditional country garden perennial: very suitable as a central plant for perennial borders. It fits with lupins, delphiniums or sages. Cut flowers last for a long time in a vase if cut as buds or when half-opened.

■ CARE NOTE: The plants like growing in the same place for a long time. They need three to four years and enough space to unfold to their full beauty. Starting from spring of the second year, you can add a low-nitrogen fertilizer and a supply of Thomas meal and potash in the fall. If you remove some buds, the others ripen to particularly big flowers.

■ PROPAGATION: The tuberous roots should be cut into 'eyes' in the early fall and should only be planted approximately 12 inches deep.

■ SPECIAL CHARACTERISTICS: All plant parts can cause nausea if eaten.

■ VARIETY TIP: 'Sarah Bernhardt' is an old variety with big, fragrant pale pink double flowers, which have a silvery glimmer. 'Raspberry Sundae' attracts attention with its fragrant, double, raspberry-pink flowers with yellow and pink centers.

Paeonia 'Madame Stuart Low'
Tree peony

▬ FAMILY: *Paeoniaceae*

▬ ORIGIN: Cultivation. The wild form comes from Bhutan, Tibet and northwestern China. The varieties belong to the *paeonia suffruticosa* group (syn. *P. suffruticosa*).

▬ GROWTH: 40 – 60 inches high; upright, thinly branched.

▬ FOLIAGE AND FLOWERS: Double-pinnate, egg-shaped, pointed leaflets; foliage is dark green on the top side, blue-green on the bottom side. Big, semi-double, intensely pink flowers with a silky glimmer and golden-yellow stamens. Flowering period is from May to June.

▬ SITE: Sunny and warm; nutrient-rich, moist, loose soil.

▬ USE: The large-flowered ornamental shrub is suitable for perennial beds and borders. It is best to grow it as a solitary or central plant. The flowers last in a vase for a long time if cut as buds or half-open.

■ CARE NOTE: Protect this perennial from frost in first winter after planting; late frosts can damage young shoots. Remove seed capsules.

■ PROPAGATION: Varieties can be sowed in summer, but they need several years to flower. Varieties are grafted. The planting time is in the fall; grafts should be 4 – 6 inches deep in the soil.

■ SPECIAL CHARACTERISTICS: Botanically speaking, tree peonies are woody shrubs, but they are often considered perennials for gardening purposes.

■ VARIETY TIP: There are single and double varieties in pink, red, white and yellow shades. 'Souvenir de Ducher' has big, globular, carmine flowers. The purple-violet flowers of 'Chinese Dragon' sit over green leaves with bronze-colored tips. 'Yoshinogawa' has pink, semi-double flowers.

Panicum virgatum 'Rotstrahlbusch'
Switchgrass

■ FAMILY: *Poaceae*

■ ORIGIN: Cultivation. This plant, also known as prairie switchgrass or tall panic grass, is widespread from Canada to California and Mexico.

■ GROWTH: 50 inches high; erect flower stalks stand out from the foliage.

■ FOLIAGE AND FLOWERS: Linear, reed-like, upright to slightly arching foliage; foliage is green with a brown glimmer and turns red in the early fall. Short, brownish spikes sit in fine, loose panicles. Flowering period is from July to September.

■ SITE: Sunny; in nutrient-rich, deep, loamy, moderately dry to moist and loose soil.

■ USE: Tall, solitary grass for perennial beds and borders, lawns and heath gardens, or pond banks. It grows in plant containers on terraces and balconies where it can protect your pri-

vacy. The fine panicles are an attractive color in the fall and are beautiful cut or dried.

■ CARE NOTE: Frosted grass is a nice decoration in winter and that is why it is better not to cut it back until spring. In summer, potted grasses must be watered and fertilized regularly.

■ PROPAGATION: Sow inside in late winter or divide in spring.

■ VARIETY TIP: 'Hänse Herms' turns brown-red in August and, by fall, it is coppery-red (foliage 25 inches, flowers 30 inches). The whole 'Heavy Metal' is blue-green and grows to a height of 50 inches. 'Rehbraun' distinguishes itself by the attractive brown color of its leaves and stalks (25 - 30 inches).

Papaver orientale
Oriental poppy

Site:
☼

Environment:
B F

Characteristics:
✂ !

■ FAMILY: *Papaveraceae*

■ ORIGIN: The species comes from Central Asia.

■ GROWTH: 10 – 40 inches high; spreads in tufts, wiry flower stalks stand out from the bushy foliage mop.

■ FOLIAGE AND FLOWERS: Pinnate, deeply divided leaves; green, silver-haired foliage. The big, orange-red, saucer-shaped flowers have a black spot at the bottom. They sit on long flower stalks. Flowering period is from May to July, depending on variety.

■ SITE: Sunny and warm; nutrient-rich, loose, deep and moderately dry soil.

■ USE: A colorful plant for beds and borders, it also likes warm southern walls. It forms a pretty group together with catmint, lupin, delphinium, false sunflower or sneezeweed. If cut as buds, the flowers last in a vase for a long time.

CARE   NOTE:
Since the poppy draws
in after flowering, it is
best to plant it in the
middle or in the back of
a flowerbed. It does not
like replanting. Damp,
cold winters often result
in rotting. Cutting back
after flowering promotes
reflowering in the fall.

PROPAGATION:
Sow in spring; cut 3 inch
long root shoots in the late fall.

SPECIAL CHARACTERISTICS: When cutting the plant,
you should be very careful because the stalks contain a poisonous milky juice.

VARIETY TIP: 'Abu Hassan' attracts attention with its
frayed, pink petals; 'Beauty of Livermere' has deep scarlet
flowers. 'Lambada' has white flowers with red margins and
a compact height of 25 inches. The white flowers of
'Perry's White' are black underneath.

Pennisetum alopecuroides
Chinese fountain grass

■ FAMILY: *Poaceae*

■ ORIGIN: The perennial (syn. *P. compressum*) is also known as fountain grass, Chinese pennisetum or swamp fox-tail. It is native to Korea, Japan and the Philippines.

■ GROWTH: 30 inches high; forming loose, compact tufts.

■ FOLIAGE AND FLOWERS: Narrow linear, slightly arching, gray-green foliage. Downy red-brown spikes float over the foliage. Flowering period is from July to September.

■ SITE: Sunny and warm, protected; nutrient-rich, not too dry and well-drained soil.

■ USE: This decorative ornamental grass is eye-catching as a solitary or in groups. It is suitable for perennial borders, on banks, in pure grass or heath gardens. Perennials flowering in the fall such as asters, eastern purple coneflowers or pincushion flowers make good companions. It is also a fine potted plant and the flowers are lovely in flower arrangements.

■ CARE NOTE: You can cut away dead leaves in winter; cutting back should be carried out in spring.

■ PROPAGATION: Sow in spring; divide in early summer.

■ SPECIAL CHARAC-TERISTICS: The utmost frost-resistant grass, it flow-ers reliably even in colder summers. However, it dislikes winter wetness. The flowers are decorative in winter.

■ VARIETY TIP: 'Compressum' forms red-brown spikes and attracts attention with the bright fall color of its foliage. It is 30 inches high including the flowers. 'Hameln' is only 25 inches high; 6-inch 'Little Bunny' is ideal for pots and flower boxes.

■ OTHER VARIETIES: *P. orientale* is, on the whole, more tender, but also more frost-sensitive and it is a good choice for rock gardens.

Penstemon barbatus
Beardtongue

▬ FAMILY: *Scrophulariaceae*

▬ ORIGIN: The variety comes from the southwest parts of the United States and Mexico. Numerous hybrid varieties are sold in stores.

▬ GROWTH: 40 inches high; upright, bushy, spreading tuft-like through creeping rhizomes.

▬ FOLIAGE AND FLOWERS: Oblong to egg-shaped, basal leaves, lance-shaped stalk leaves; fresh green, glossy foliage. Funnel-shaped, pink-red flowers hang loosely in narrow panicles. Flowering period is from June to September.

▬ SITE: Sunny and warm; nutrient-rich, fertile, moderately moist and loose soil.

▬ USE: A flowering perennial for sunny beds and borders. It likes growing in front of warm southern walls and is popular as a potted plant and as a cut flower. Speedwell, goldenrod, coreopsis, evening primrose, Shasta daisy or sage look very nice in its company.

■ CARE NOTE: If cut regularly for a vase, the perennial will flower again and again. Cut it back in late fall and cover with dry leaves or twigs; in cold regions, it is better to take it into the house. Hybrids are often cultivated only as annuals.

■ PROPAGATION: Sow inside in early spring. Shoots cut from late spring to summer grow quickly.

■ VARIETY TIP: 'Schönholzeri' is a hybrid variety with big, scarlet flowers resembling purple foxglove. 'Blue Springs' has gentian-blue flowers and is only 12 inches high.

■ OTHER VARIETIES: *P. digitalis* 'Husker's Red Strain' is extraordinarily decorative with white flowers and bronze foliage.

Phlox paniculata
Perennial phlox

▬ FAMILY: *Polemoniaceae*

▬ ORIGIN: The plant is also known as fall phlox or garden phlox and comes from the east coast of North America. Numerous hybrids are sold in stores.

▬ GROWTH: 15 – 50 inches high; forming large, upright tufts.

▬ FOLIAGE AND FLOWERS: Lance-shaped to narrow egg-shaped leaves; fresh green foliage. Wheel-shaped, solitary flowers sit in thick, spheric umbels. Varieties flower in red, pink, lilac or white shades. Its sweet scent is especially noticeable towards evening. Its flowering period is from July to September.

▬ SITE: Sunny; in nutrient-rich, fertile, deep, moist, but loose, neutral to slightly acidic soil. In the half-shade, it flowers later in the season.

▬ USE: A colorful bed and cut perennial, which does well in a plant container as well. Fleabane, delphinium, Shasta daisy, coreopsis or grasses make good neighbors.

■ CARE NOTE: A fertilizer or compost should be applied in spring. The flowering period will be longer if you cut back one third of its shoots in June. Winter protection is necessary in cold regions or during black frosts.

■ PROPAGATION: Cut off shoots in spring or summer; cut before or after flowering.

■ SPECIAL CHARACTERISTICS: Deformed shoots and poorer growth indicate nematode infection. Infested plants must be removed immediately.

■ VARIETY TIP: The pink flowers of 'Landhochzeit' are adorned with red eyes (50 inches). The purple flowers of 'Wenn schon, denn schon' are adorned with white eyes (35 inches). 'Blue Paradise' is a novelty with blue flowers (15 inches); 'Orange' and 'Windsor' have bright orange-red flowers (12 inches).

Phlox subulata
'Emerald Cushion Blue'
Moss phlox

▬ FAMILY: *Polemoniaceae*

▬ ORIGIN: This variety, also known as dwarf phlox, is native to North America.

▬ GROWTH: 4 – 6 inches high; forms wide, flat flower cushions.

▬ FOLIAGE AND FLOWERS: Needle-shaped, stiff, evergreen leaves; intensely green. The plant produces large displays of stellate, light violet flowers. There are red, pink, lilac and white varieties. Flowering period is from April to June.

▬ SITE: Sunny and warm; moderately nutrient-rich, fertile, sandy, loose and moderately dry soil.

▬ USE: An abundantly flowering cushion perennial for rock gardens; ideal for bordering flowerbeds, terraces and waysides. Moss phlox looks beautiful growing down walls. It is recommended for planting in troughs as well as on roof gardens because it quickly forms a thick flower carpet.

■ CARE NOTE: The plant should be protected from the bright winter sun and severe frosts.

■ PROPAGATION: Divide cushions in fall or cut shoots in spring.

■ VARIETY TIP: 'Scarlet Flame' has scarlet flowers; robust 'Temiscaming' has bright purple ones. The flowers of 'Candy Stripes' are merrily striped with white and pink. 'Violet Seedling' enchants with reddish-violet flower beauty; 'White Delight' charms with snow-white beauty.

■ OTHER VARIETIES: *P. divaricata* prefers semi-shaded sites, but it also grows in abundantly moist soil in the sun. The blue-violet 'Clouds of Perfume' and its white counterpart 'White Perfume' spread a sweet scent from April to June (both 15 inches high).

Phyllostachys aurea
Golden bamboo

Site:
☼ – ☀

Environment:
G W F

Characteristics:

▬ FAMILY: *Poaceae*

▬ ORIGIN: The natural habitat of the golden bamboo or fish pole bamboo (syn. *Bambusa aurea*) is the forest ecosystem of southern China, with its warm summers and humid air.

▬ GROWTH: 10 – 15 feet high (up to 40 feet when old); narrow and upright, slightly arching in the upper part, tufted, forming few offshoots, a woody shrub.

▬ FOLIAGE AND FLOWERS: Canes up to 1 inch in diameter with thickened lower nodules. Green, but glowing yellow in the sun. Leaves are narrow, lance-shaped and yellow-green. Evergreen as well.

▬ SITE: Sunny to semi-shaded, wind protected; nutrient-rich, fertile, moist and loose soil; bamboo tolerates dryness as well. Preferably in regions with mild winters; leaves can be damaged by a temperature of 10°F or lower; all aboveground plant parts die at -4°F.

▬ USE: The exotic giant grass can be planted on this own

in a garden or on the bank of a pond, as a hedge or bamboo grove as well as a potted plant in a conservatory. It provides natural protection of privacy.

CARE NOTE: Canes must be bound together in winter and be covered with straw mats. In cold regions, it is recommended that you cover the root area with dry leaves, sacking or straw. If protected from drying winds and winter sun, the plant tolerates frosts better. Potted plants should be fertilized every month during their growing period.

PROPAGATION: Divide in spring or in fall.

OTHER VARIETIES: From the second year of growth, the canes of the black-jointed bamboo *(P. nigra)* are brown or black.

Platycodon grandiflorus
Balloon flower

FAMILY: *Campanulaceae*

ORIGIN: The sole species of the genus comes from East Asia.

GROWTH: 20 inches high; upright, bushy, with beet-like, thickened roots.

FOLIAGE AND FLOWERS: Egg or lance-shaped leaves, toothed at margins; intensely green to bluish-green foliage. Bright blue, stellate, bell-shaped flowers develop from balloon-like buds. Other varieties can be white or pink. Flowering period is from July to August.

SITE: Sunny to semi-shaded; nutrient-rich, fertile, well-drained and moderately moist soil.

USE: This easy-to-grow perennial is a colorful eye-catcher in loose perennial groups, rock gardens, along the edges of woody plants and in rose beds as well as bowls and flower boxes. Astilbes, meadow sweet, evening primrose, carnations, blazing star, pincushion flowers and grasses such as switchgrass

Site:
☼ – ☼

Environment:
B S G F

Characteristics:

combine harmoniously with it. Taller varieties can be used as cut flowers.

▬ CARE NOTE: Since this perennial blooms late, its planting places should be marked and the plant should be combined with evergreen or early sprouting partners. It can be cut greatly back between late fall and late winter. Once settled, the plants like growing without being disturbed.

▬ PROPAGATION: Sow in spring.

▬ VARIETY TIP: 'Fuji White' (pure white), 'Fuji Blue' (dark blue) and 'Fuji Pink' (pink) have particularly large-flowers. 'Album' has white flowers with light blue veins; the big flowers of 'Mariesii' are lilac-blue. The blue 'Zwerg' is very low-growing with a height of 6 inches.

Polypodium vulgare
Common polypody

▬ FAMILY: *Polypodiaceae*

▬ ORIGIN: The protected common polypody is native in northern, temperate zones, but it can be found in the African continent too. Many people know it as 'female fern' or 'sweet fern'.

▬ GROWTH: 8 inches high; upright to arching, spreading through creeping rhizomes.

▬ FOLIAGE: Pinnate fronds, narrow, triangular, leathery, with distinctive pimply undersides (the spore-bearing organs); evergreen; dark green.

▬ SITE: Preferably shady, also semi-shaded; fertile, moderately dry to moist and acid soil.

▬ USE: A small fern for the shadiest places in a garden or rock garden. It likes growing in the shade of dry walls or in wall or stone cracks. Since it rarely grows rampantly, it can be combined with other shade perennials: lily of the valley, lady fern, crested shield fern or nodding melick. It is also recommended for planting in troughs and flower boxes.

■ CARE NOTE: This fern prefers growing in the same place for years without being disturbed - as do all ferns.

■ PROPAGATION: Sow or divide in early spring.

■ VARIETY TIP: 'Bifidum Multifidum' attracts attention with its reddish, deeply split fronds branched like tassels. Its compact height of 15 inches is suitable for small gardens and plant containers.

■ OTHER VARIETIES: Intermediate polypody *(P. interjectum)* has very pinnate, finely divided fronds. The 10-inch variety 'Cornubiense' is often sold in stores.

Polystichum tsus-simense
Korean rock fern

▬ FAMILY: Dryopteridaceae

▬ ORIGIN: The extensive genus is widespread in Alpine and tropical regions. This variety is native to China, Korea, Japan and Taiwan.

▬ GROWTH: Up to 15 inches high; narrow, fronds arranged like rosettes on erect rhizomes, like shuttlecocks.

▬ FOLIAGE: Fronds are double pinnate, broadly lance-shaped, individual pinnas are pointed and serrated at margins; dull, dark green.

▬ SITE: Semi-shaded to shady, humid air; nutrient-rich, fertile and moist soil.

▬ USE: The tender fern can be planted in shady areas of a rock garden or in pots in shady courtyards, or on terraces and balconies. It is very appealing in combination with other shade perennials such as European columbines, Japanese thimble-weeds, astilbes, primroses or shade grasses.

CARE NOTE: The variety is hardy only in temperate regions. In cold regions, the plant must be protected. It is best for it to spend the winter in a cool, bright room.

PROPAGATION: You can get new plants quickly by dividing bigger specimens in spring.

OTHER VARIETIES:

P. setiferum is a robust hardy, variety with many names; it is also known as 'soft shield fern,' 'English hedge fern' or 'hedge fern.' 'Plumosum Densum' is only about 15 inches high and grows like a wide funnel. The triple pinnate fronds (with slightly curly and overlapping pinnas) are light green to bronze-green. 'Dahlem' is approximately 30 inches high with broad, almost upright fronds; 'Herrenhausen' is 15 inches, has long fronds and grows so wide that it is almost flat. The hard shield-fern *(P. aculeatum)* has stout leathery, glossy green, double pinnate fronds and even tolerates sunny places.

Primula denticulata
Drumstick primula

Site:

Environment:
S G F

Characteristics:

■ FAMILY: *Primulaceae*

■ ORIGIN: Wild plants are widespread in the highlands of Afghanistan and western China as well as in the Himalayas.

■ GROWTH: 12 – 15 inches high; upright, firm flowers followed by a basal foliage rosette.

■ FOLIAGE AND FLOWERS: Dull green, spoon-shaped, crinkly leaves, finely serrated at margins. The globular flowers consists of numerous, tiny, bell-shaped flowers. This variety is lilac- colored, but the color spectrum of all the varieties ranges from white, pink and red to lilac. Flowering period is from March to May.

■ SITE: Semi-shaded to shady; fertile, moist but loose soil. Also likes a sunny site, but only in abundantly moist soil.

■ USE: A colorful spring flower for shadier rock gardens and under woody plants such as rhododendrons. Particularly beautiful in small groups of various colors. The primrose is among the first plants to flower in bowls, flower boxes and flower arrangements. Other spring flowers such as hyacinths, tulips, violets, forget-me-nots, ferns or grasses, make good companions.

▬ Propagation: Sow in spring; divide plants after flowering, or cut root shoots in winter.

▬ Variety tip: 'Alba' has pure white flowers; 'Rubin' is carmine. 'Grandiflora' is a mixture of lilac, violet and pink shades.

▬ Other varieties: The fragrant 8 inch high cowslip *(P. veris)* flowers in light yellow from April to May. It is a popular wild perennial for natural and rock gardens; its orange-red eye attracts insects.

Primula japonica
Japanese primrose

Site:
☀ – ☀

Environment:
W G S

Characteristics:

■ FAMILY: *Primulaceae*

■ ORIGIN: Japan and Taiwan, at heights above 11,500 feet in moist meadows or in slightly wooded swamp areas.

■ GROWTH: 15 – 20 inches high; upright, firm flowers stalks stand out from a basal foliage rosette.

■ FOLIAGE AND FLOWERS: Oblong to spoon-shaped light green leaves with uneven or serrated margins. Carmine flowers, arranged in whorls; varieties are also pink and white. Flowering period is from June to July.

■ SITE: Semi-shaded to shady; fertile, loamy, acid and moist to wet soil. Also in a sunny location, but only in very moist soil.

■ USE: The perennial likes growing near water, in marshy soil or in the shade of shrubs and trees. It is recommended for moist areas in rock gardens and does well in plant containers if the soil is continuously moist. European columbine, anemones,

liverworts, violets, ferns or shade grasses are pretty companions for primroses.

■■■ PROPAGATION: Sow in spring. Plants should be divided after flowering so that the color of the flowers is preserved.

■■■ VARIETY TIP: 'Alba' has beautiful white flowers, while 'Atropurpurea' and 'Millers Crimson' are a rich carmine color. The white flowers of 'Postford White' have red eyes.

■■■ OTHER VARIETIES: Another Japanese primrose is *P. bulleyana* (candelabra primrose), whose orange-red to yellow, fragrant flower whorls appear in July-August. The giant cowslip or Tibetan primrose *(P. florindae)* impresses with its softly fragrant, yellow glowing corymbs in June – August. It is 25 – 35 inches high and requires consistently moist soil.

Pulsatilla vulgaris
Pasque flower

▬ FAMILY: *Ranunculaceae*

▬ ORIGIN: The common pasque flower is native to Europe and is protected.

▬ GROWTH: 8 inches high; forms tufts from robust rhizomes.

▬ FOLIAGE AND FLOWERS: Multiple pinnate, fern-like leaves: initially silvery-haired, dull green later. Big, bell-shaped flowers are upright or nodding at ends of stalks. The yellow stamens contrast with the outer, downy haired petals. The petals of this variety are blue-violet; other varieties are also red, pink or white. Flowering period is from April to May.

▬ SITE: Sunny to semi-shaded, warm; moderately nutrient-rich, loose and limy soil.

▬ USE: A splendid spring flower for rock gardens or steppe heaths. Inula, Italian aster, pussytoes, common yarrow, sunrose, dwarf iris, festuca or needle grass are good companions for it. The pasque flower also does well in pots.

▬ CARE NOTE: The perennial dislikes cold, damp weather.

▬ PROPAGATION: The seeds must be sowed as soon as they are ripe because they lose their ability to germinate quickly. Divide plants in spring or cut root shoots after flowering, but remember: the plants do not like being disturbed.

▬ SPECIAL CHARACTERISTICS: The flowers are a popular nectar source for insects. They are followed by fruits with long silvery hairs that last until summer. If eaten, the plant causes nausea. The plant juice irritates the skin.

▬ VARIETY TIP: 'Alba' has off-white flowers, 'Pink Shades' is pink, 'Rote Glocke' (syn. 'Rode Klokke') and 'Rubra' flower in bright red shades. 'Papageno' is a mixture of all colors.

Ranunculus acris 'Multiplex'
Double meadow buttercup

■ FAMILY: *Ranunculaceae*

■ ORIGIN: Cultivation. The wild form, the protected buttercup, is native to Europe, the Caucasus and western Siberia. It has been brought to North America and naturalized.

■ GROWTH: 25 inches high; upright, bushy, spreads in tufts through short offshoots, but does not grow rampantly.

■ FOLIAGE AND FLOWERS: Fresh green, palmate leaves, serrated at the margins. Double, pompon, golden-yellow flowers sit at the ends of branched flowers stalks over the foliage. Flowering period is from May to June.

■ SITE: Sunny to semi-shaded; inutrient-rich, moderately moist to moist soil.

■ USE: A popular perennial for banks, perennial meadows and natural gardens; also suitable for borders and as a cut flower. It is best to plant it in groups. European columbine, meadow sweet, field balm or globe flower complete the picture.

■ CARE NOTE: The double meadow buttercup cannot grow in very dry soil.

■ PROPAGATION: Divide in spring or in the fall. Sow directly after the seeds have ripened; the germination of older seeds is lengthy.

■ SPECIAL CHARACTERISTICS: A poisonous plant. All plant parts cause nausea if eaten.

■ OTHER VARIETIES: The white water crowfoot *(R. aquatilis)* with floating leaves is an easy-to-grow plant for garden ponds. Saucer-shaped, white flowers with yellow centers appear on the surface of the water in summer.

Rodgersia pinnata 'Superba'
Rodger's flower

Site:
☀ – ☀

Environment:
G W

 FAMILY: *Saxifragaceae*

 ORIGIN: The variety grows in the mountainous forests of the Chinese province Yunnan.

 GROWTH: 60 inches high; upright, loosely bushy, forming tufts through flat, creeping rhizomes.

 FOLIAGE AND FLOWERS: Big, digitate, crinkly, veined leaves, similar those of a chestnut tree: bronze in spring, scarlet in fall. Pyramidal, feathery panicles with numerous small pink flowers are carried by robust, reddish stems. Flowering period is from June to July.

 SITE: Semi-shaded to shady, wind protected; fertile, loamy, moist soil.

 USE: A decorative perennial for woody plant edges and banks. It fits particularly well with coniferous trees or rhododendrons; astilbes, monkshood, snakeroot, wide-leaved bellflower, ferns and shade grasses are also fine companions.

■■■ CARE NOTE: The plant prefers slightly dryer soil in the shade and generally does not tolerate humidity.

■■■ PROPAGATION: Divide or sow in spring (moist moss is the best substrate).

■■■ OTHER CHARACTERISTICS: The flowers are followed by dark-red seed capsules.

■■■ VARIETY TIP: 'Elegans' enchants with yellowish white panicles.

■■■ OTHER VARIETIES: The ornamental leaves (bronze-colored when sprouting) of *R. podophylla* 'Rotlaub' can reach a diameter of 20 inches. The yellowish white flower panicles contrast marvelously with them.

Rudbeckia fulgida var. *sullivantii* 'Goldsturm'
Black-eyed Susan

■ FAMILY: *Asteraceae*

■ ORIGIN: Cultivation. The species (syn. *R. sullivantii*) is native to North America; the commonest variant is also known as orange coneflower.

■ GROWTH: 25 inches high; wide, bushy foliage, tufted, spreads through runners.

■ FOLIAGE AND FLOWERS: Big basal leaves, broadly elliptic, smaller, lance-shaped, rough and hairy stalk leaves; dark green. Daisy flowers with golden-yellow, stellate petals and black eyes. Flowering period is from July to September.

■ SITE: Sunny; in nutrient-rich, moderately moist, loose soil.

■ USE: This sparkling summer perennial with a long flowering period is great in all sunny perennial beds and borders. Its compact form makes it ideal for planting in pots so that it can be enjoyed on the terrace or balcony as well. The flowers and fruits

are a pretty decoration for late summer flower arrangements. Asters, delphinium or sage are good companions.

▬ CARE NOTE: This easy-care perennial dislikes dryness. If dead flowers are not immediately cut off, they make a pretty decoration in winter.

▬ PROPAGATION: Divide in spring. Replant every five or six years for best results.

▬ OTHER VARIETIES: Double, pompon, lemon-yellow flowers distinguish *R. laciniata* 'Goldquelle' from the described rudbeckia. *R. nitida* 'Herbstsonne' with simple yellow flowers grows easily to a height of 80 inches.

Salvia nemorosa
Sage

■ FAMILY: *Lamiaceae*

■ ORIGIN: This fragrant perennial is widespread and grows wild from eastern Central Europe to Southwest Asia.

■ GROWTH: 15 – 25 inches high; some varieties are even taller; upright, bushy, spreading through tufts.

■ FOLIAGE AND FLOWERS: Lance-shaped, crinkly, fragrant; dull green foliage. Tubular, two-lipped flowers sit in slender, candle-like spikes. Varieties are blue, violet, pink and white. Flowering period is from May to September.

■ SITE: Sunny and warm; nutrient-rich, loose and moderately dry soil.

■ USE: A long-flowering plant for beds, borders and rock gardens, it is also suitable for greening sunny slopes as well as for planting in flower containers and boxes. It does well in the company of roses, coreopsis, medium coneflowers or baby's breath.

━━ CARE NOTE: If the perennial is cut back by one-third after flowering, it flowers again in the fall. Cutting back at the ground level in spring ensures a willing sprouting of the plant. The plant should be protected from wetness and drying wind in winter.

━━ PROPAGATION: Divide or sow in spring; shoots can be cut in summer as well. If the plant is healthy, it sets seeds abundantly on its own.

━━ SPECIAL NOTES: Bees and bumblebees like romping on the long spikes.

━━ VARIETY TIP: 'Blauhügel' has pure blue flowers; 'Mainacht' has dark violet-blue ones. The dark violet flowers on almost black stalks are a specialty of 'Caradonna.' 'Rosakönigin' contributes with pink-red flowers; 'Rubin' is red, 'Adrian' and 'Schneehügel' are white.

Salvia sclarea
Biennial clary sage

▬ FAMILY: *Lamiaceae*

▬ ORIGIN: The plant is widespread in southern and Eastern Europe, North Africa and central Asia.

▬ GROWTH: 40 inches high; upright, richly branched foliage; biennial, i.e. the big foliage rosette appears in the first year after sowing, flower candles appear the following year.

▬ FOLIAGE AND FLOWERS: Lance-shaped, up to 8 inch long, crinkly, hairy, and strongly fragrant leaves; mid-green. The candle-like flowers consist of numerous cream-white to pink or lilac-colored, solitary flowers. Flowering period is from June to August.

▬ SITE: Sunny, warm and wind protected; nutrient-rich, loose and moderately dry soil.

▬ USE: A charming flower perennial for the background of beds and also borders. Its beauty is highlighted if it is planted as a solitary or in a flower container.

■ PROPAGATION: Seeds are sowed directly outdoors or in pots and boxes starting in May. They should be covered slightly with soil. The soil must be kept moist; winter protection must be provided in cold regions. The plant self-seeds in favorable places.

■ SPECIAL CHARACTERISTICS: While the flowers are frequently visited by bees and bumblebees, the musky leaves add a special touch to meals and cosmetic preparations. If dried, they can be put into fragrant pillows. The essential oil can be used as an aphrodisiac preparation.

■ OTHER VARIETIES: The meadow sage (*S. pratensis* subsp. *haematodes*), native to Europe, complements the clary sage. The tightly packed panicles of the variety 'Mittsommer' glimmer in light lavender-blue from June to August (30 inches high).

Santolina chamaecyparissus
Cotton lavender

▬ FAMILY: *Asteraceae*

▬ ORIGIN: The perennial, also called santolina, can be found growing in the Mediterranean region.

▬ GROWTH: 15 inches high; bushy branched, forms rounded cushions, a woody semi-shrub at the crown.

▬ FOLIAGE AND FLOWERS: Finely pinnate, evergreen, aromatically fragrant foliage with silver-gray hairs. Small golden-yellow heads sit at the ends of stalks. Flowering period is from July to August.

▬ SITE: Sunny and warm; nutrient-rich, loose, dry and limy soil.

▬ USE: This sun-lover likes growing in dry and warm places whether in a rock garden or along southern walls. Since it is easy to cut it to achieve a nice form, it can be used to border rose beds in regions with mild winters. The gray foliage contrasts nicely with almost every flower color. If you plant it in a flower container or box, you can bring its sweet scent nearer to you.

■ Care note: Annual cutting back maintains the plant's shape. Winter protection is recommended in colder regions.

■ Propagation: Shoots cut from late spring to summer grow to young plants quickly.

■ Special character-istics: The fine gray hairs protect the leaves from extreme evaporation in warm sites.

■ Variety tip: 'Edward Bowles' has cream-white flowers over gray-green foliage (15 inches).

■ Other varieties: The green lavender cotton *(S. rosmarinifolia)* is adorned with soft green leaves and sulfur-yellow flowers.

Saxifraga x arendsii
Rockfoil

■ FAMILY: *Saxifragaceae*

■ ORIGIN: Cultivation. The parent varieties of mossy saxifrage come mostly from temperate mountainous regions.

■ GROWTH: 1 – 6 inches high – depending on type; moss-like flower cushions.

■ FOLIAGE AND FLOWERS: Lance-shaped, pinnatifid, evergreen, intensively green foliage. Tender saucer-shaped flowers stand out from the cushions on thin, branched stalks. They are pink, red or white depending on the variety. Flowering period is from April to May.

■ SITE: Semi-shaded; nutrient-rich, fertile, loose and moderately dry soil.

■ USE: A low-maintenance spring flower for rock gardens. It looks pretty growing down walls. It can be planted at waysides or along staircases, on graves as well as in flower boxes and troughs. European columbine, bergenia, barrenwort, primroses, alumroot and dwarf bleeding heart complete the picture.

▬ Care note: The plant does not like humidity.

▬ Propagation: The cushions can be divided in spring. Small, unrooted rosettes cut in the fall can be propagated under glass like shoots.

▬ Variety tip: 'Purpurteppich' impresses with plenty of dark wine flowers; 'Schneeteppich' is white. Red shades are offered by 'Blütenteppich' (carmine) and 'Ingeborg' (dark red). The pink 'Birch Baby' and the white 'Schneezwerg' are very low (1 inch).

▬ Other varieties: *S. x apiculata* impresses with a yellow flower cushion over evergreen foliage rosettes from March to April.

Scabiosa caucasica
Pincushion flower

■ FAMILY: *Dipsacaceae*

■ ORIGIN: This variety comes from the Caucasus.

■ GROWTH: 25 – 35 inches high based on the variety; bushy, tufted.

■ FOLIAGE AND FLOWERS: Lance-shaped, gray green basal leaves, pinnatifid stalk leaves. The big, saucer-shaped heads with curly petals sit on erect, sometimes branched stalks. There are blue, blue-violet or white varieties. Flowering period is from June to September.

■ SITE: Sunny, warm and protected; nutrient-rich, limy, loose and moderately moist soil.

■ USE: The pincushion flowers enrich beds and borders with their tender floral beauty. They are also durable cut flowers and grow in flower containers on sunny balconies. They do well in the company of roses, asters, fleabanes, sages, yarrows and rudbeckias.

▬ CARE NOTE: The perennial is very sensitive to wetness and frost. On that note, it must be protected and covered in winter. It is cut back greatly in late winter so that it will sprout again.

▬ PROPAGATION: Sow or divide in early spring; cut basal shoots from late spring to early summer.

▬ SPECIAL CHARACTERISTICS: Flowers of the pincushion flower are very popular with bees and butterflies.

▬ VARIETY TIP: 'Blauer Atlas' has deep blue flowers; 'Clive Greaves' is light blue. The flowers of 'Miss E. Willmott' are pure white; flowers of 'Stäfa' are dark violet.

Sedum acre
Biting stonecrop

Site:
☼

Environment:
S F

Characteristics:

- FAMILY: *Crassulaceae*

- ORIGIN: Native to Europe, naturalized in North America.

- GROWTH: 2 - 4 inches high; forms carpets with creeping stalks, spreads abundantly.

- FOLIAGE AND FLOWERS: Green cylindrical, fleshy, evergreen leaves. The foliage cushion is dotted with stellate, bright yellow flowers. Flowering period is from June to July.

- SITE: Sunny, dry; moderately nutrient-rich, sandy and loose soil.

- USE: A plant for the driest areas of a garden. A must for a rock garden and dry walls, recommended for exposed roof gardens, gravel gardens and for planting in graves and troughs. The perennial immediately covers bare places. It can grow in the company of other cushion perennials – maiden pink, creeping thyme or festuca.

■ CARE NOTE: The modest succulent stores water in its leaves and therefore tolerates very dry soil and warm weather, but it is capable of spreading more than you may want it to.

■ PROPAGATION: The plants set seed by themselves and can be divided in spring.

■ SPECIAL CHARACTERISTICS: A poisonous plant. The consumption of the shoots and the very hot leaves can cause nausea. But the nectar-rich flowers are very popular among insects.

■ VARIETY TIP: 'Aureum' not only has yellow flowers, but also yellow leaves. 'Minor' is only 2 inches high.

■ OTHER VARIETIES: *S. kamtschaticum* 'Variegatum' has glowing yellow flowers which later turn red. The spoon-shaped leaves are decorated with a yellowish edge.

Sedum spectabile 'Brillant'
Ice plant

■ FAMILY: *Crassulaceae*

■ ORIGIN: Cultivation. The variety, also called showy stonecrop, comes originally from Korea and China.

■ GROWTH: 15 inches high; bushy, upright, forming tufts.

■ FOLIAGE AND FLOWERS: Broadly elliptic, fleshy foliage, gray-green toothed at the margins. Every umbrella-shaped flowers comprises a great variety of small, stellate, dark pink flowers perched on the ends of firm, smooth, non-branched flowers stalks. Flowering period is from August to September.

■ SITE: Sunny and warm; nutrient-rich, constantly moist and loose soil.

■ USE: The late flowering succulent fits particularly well at edges of perennial beds, in front of warm southern walls, in rock gardens, flower containers and boxes. Grasses, bushy asters and sages are its companions in late summer. The flowers can be used as cut flowers.

■ CARE NOTE: Unlike the other sedum varieties, the soil should not dry out here. A compost addition in spring will be rewarded by rich flowering.

■ PROPAGATION: Divide at the beginning of growth in spring.

■ SPECIAL CHARAC-TERISTICS: The wide flower

umbrellas are favorite meeting points for bees and other insects collecting nectar. The brown fruits are a pretty decoration until winter.

■ VARIETY TIP: The carmine 'Brillant' is one of the most popular varieties. 'Carmen' has dark pink flowers and also tolerates dryness. 'Frosty Morn' carries carmine flowers over white-green foliage. 'Stardust' has white flowers.

■ OTHER VARIETIES: *S. telephium* 'Herbstfreude,' whose rust-colored flowers bloom until October, is a classic.

Sempervivum-Hybrids
Houseleek

Site:
☼

Environment:
S F B

Characteristics:
〰〰➤

▬ FAMILY: *Crassulaceae*

▬ ORIGIN: Cultivation. The varieties of this extensive genus can be found in the mountainous regions of Europe and Asia.

▬ GROWTH: Up to 4 inches high; flat, broad or small bud-like rosettes spread in the form of a cushion.

▬ FOLIAGE AND FLOWERS: Elliptic, pointed, fleshy, symmetrically arranged in rosettes; light to black-green or reddish to brown, sometimes with silver foliage hairs depending on the variety. The coloration of the leaves is particularly intense in spring. Corymbs with small, stellate flowers, in pink, red, yellow or white shades depending on the variety, sit on upright flowers stalks. Flowering period is mostly from June to July.

▬ SITE: Sunny, dry; nutrient-rich, sandy, loose and dry soil.

▬ USE: An evergreen succulent for sunny places in rock gardens. It grows in wall cracks, gravel beds, on roof gardens

and is suitable for edges as well as for graves. Low bearded irises, stonecrop and rockfoil varieties, pussytoes or thymes can be used as its neighbors. You can have a collection of numerous varieties in bowls and flower boxes as well.

▬ CARE NOTE: The plant tolerates very dry soil, hardly needs any nutrients and requires only a small place. Heavily haired plants should be protected from winter wetness.

▬ PROPAGATION: Young rosettes can be separated from spring to summer. If they do not have roots, they are treated like shoots.

▬ VARIETY TIP: 'Black Prince,' for lovers of dark shade, can be planted (black-purple leaves with green tips) or 'Noir' (black-green with red tips).

Silene x arkwrightii 'Orange Zwerg'
Arkwright's campion

▬ FAMILY: *Carypophyllaceae*

▬ ORIGIN: Cultivation. The variety hybrid is also well-known as *Lychnis x arkwrightii*; and was registered under this name for years.

▬ GROWTH: 12 inches high; upright, loosely bushy, tufted.

▬ FOLIAGE AND FLOWERS: Egg to lance-shaped green leaves draw in after flowering. Several stellate, five-petal, bright orange flowers sit at the end of stalks. Flowering period is from June to July-August.

▬ SITE: Preferably sunny, but also semi-shaded; nutrient-rich, loose, but sufficiently moist soil.

▬ USE: A richly flowering border perennial, which ensures glowing color effects visible from far away if planted in groups. The flowers can be cut and put into a vase.

▬ CARE NOTE: The removal of dead flowers helps prolong the flowering period. The perennials rot slightly in wet, winter soil.

▬ PROPAGATION: Divide after flowering or sow in spring.

▬ VARIETY TIP: 'Vesuvius' carries glowing, orange-red flowers over dark brown-red leaves (15 inches).

▬ OTHER VARIETIES: The Maltese cross (*S. chalcedonica*, syn. *Lychnis chalcedonica*) is a glowing, red flowerbed perennial found for centuries in country gardens. It grows up to 40 inches high. The German catchfly (*S. viscaria*, syn. *Lychnis viscaria*) has purple-red flowers; the variety 'Plena' has double flowers.

Solidago-Hybride 'Tara'
Goldenrod

Site:
☼

Environment:
B F

Characteristics:
✄

▬ FAMILY: *Asteraceae*

▬ ORIGIN: Cultivation. The parent varieties come from North America.

▬ GROWTH: 30 inches high; upright, bushy, tufted, grows hardily, but not rampantly.

▬ FOLIAGE AND FLOWERS: Oblong to lance-shaped, distinctly veined, fresh-green leaves. Very small, glowing, yellow, stellate flowers float in thick panicles over the foliage. Flowering period is from July to September.

▬ SITE: Sunny; moderately nutrient-rich, loamy and moist soil.

▬ USE: A striking flowering perennial for beds and borders, very pretty in a wild flower garden. It flowers again in late summer together with New England asters, chrysanthemums, fleabanes, delphiniums, pincushion flowers or sneezeweeds. Goldenrods provide durable cut flowers.

■ CARE NOTE: Dead flower stalks should be cut away in time so that the plant does not set seed on its own.

■ PROPAGATION: You get new plants most quickly through dividing in spring. This also ensures regeneration of the perennial at the same time.

■ SPECIAL CHARACTERISTICS: The flowers are a welcomed nectar source for bees and other insects in late summer.

■ VARIETY TIP: Golden-yellow, mimosa-like flowers are a characteristic of 'Goldenmosa.' 'Strahlenkrone' forms flat, golden-yellow panicles. 'Ledsham' has light yellow flowers.

■ OTHER VARIETIES: *x Solidaster* luteus is a hybrid of the *Aster ptarmicoides* and *Solidago*. Its light yellow, daisy-like flowers sit in thick clusters and are suitable for flower arrangements.

Stachys byzantina
Lambs' ears

■ FAMILY: *Lamiaceae*

■ ORIGIN: The variety (syn. *S. lanata*) coming from West Asia is also known as 'bunnies' ears,' 'woolly betony' or 'woundwort.'

■ GROWTH: 12 inches high; upright, bushy, forming tufts through off-shoots.

■ FOLIAGE AND FLOWERS: Oblong to elliptic, firm, basal leaves are arranged like in rosettes; gray-white foliage, densely covered in white fuzz. Slender, spiky, woolly pink flowers. Flowering period is from July to September.

■ SITE: Sunny to semi-shaded, protected from wetness; in nutrient-rich and sandy soil.

■ USE: The silver-leaf perennial lights up dark and dry areas in a garden. It can also be used for borders. It forms a lovely interplay of colors together with bergenias, hostas, lady's mantles, common bugles, catmints or roses.

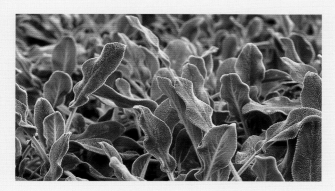

■ CARE NOTE: The plants rot slightly in wet soil during the winter.

■ PROPAGATION: Divide in early spring.

■ SPECIAL CHARACTERISTICS: Bees and other insects like the flowers, but they are rather unattractive to people.

■ VARIETY TIP: 'Silver Carpet' is only 6 inches high and greens even larger areas with its thick, flat carpets. The modest plant hardly flowers and is suitable for graves.

■ OTHER VARIETIES: *S. macrantha* 'Superba' (syn. *S. grandiflora*) grows upright to a height of 25 inches and enchants with purple flowers in whorls.

Stipa tenacissima
Needle grass

Site:
☼

Environment:
F S

Characteristics:
 ✄

■ FAMILY: *Poaceae*

■ ORIGIN: The variety native to China is also known as esparto grass or Mexican feather grass.

■ GROWTH: 25 inches high; loosely tufted, with long, arching, flower blades.

■ FOLIAGE AND FLOWERS: Narrow, long, rolled, light green foliage. Greenish-white spikes with long awns are divided into big, feathery panicles. Flowering period is from July to August.

■ SITE: Sunny, dry; nutrient-rich, sandy and loamy soil.

■ USE: A graceful ornamental grass whose beauty is highlighted if it is planted as a solitary. A good choice for wild flower gardens, rock gardens, terraced gardens, grass communities and surrounding garden ponds. The stalks are popular with florists. They must be cut at the right time in order to last in a vase.

▬ CARE NOTE: The plant dislikes longer rainy periods especially in winter, and it prefers some protection. It should be cut back greatly in spring.

▬ PROPAGATION: Divide in spring as soon as the growth begins or sow in the fall.

▬ SPECIAL CHARACTERISTICS: The tender flower blades move even with the gentlest wind. A fibrous textile material is produced from the leaves.

▬ OTHER VARIETIES: European feather grass *(S. pennata)*, with its height of 15 inches, is more compact and fits particularly well in plant containers or bigger flower boxes.

Thymus x citriodorus
Lemon thyme

▬ FAMILY: *Lamiaceae*

▬ ORIGIN: A hybrid of the golden-scented thyme *(T. pulegioides)* and the common thyme *(T. vulgaris).* The varieties are native to Europe; *T. vulgaris* is native to the Mediterranean region.

▬ GROWTH: 6 inches high; forms plump cushions.

▬ FOLIAGE AND FLOWERS: Elliptic to lance-shaped, narrow, evergreen foliage; yellow-green, lemon-scented leaves. Small, two-lipped, light pink flowers sit in loose clusters. Flowering period is from June to July.

▬ SITE: Sunny and warm; moderately nutrient-rich to infertile, sandy, loose and dry soil.

▬ USE: An aromatic perennial for rock and heath gardens as well as for troughs and flower boxes. It looks very decorative along borders or in cracks of pathways and staircases. The aromatic leaves are often used for seasoning meals and they complement herb beds.

■■■ CARE NOTE: Cutting back after flowering or in spring preserves the growth intensity. The plants rot in excessively moist soil in winter. Besides, the plant should be protected from frost with a dry cover, such as pine branches.

■■■ PROPAGATION: Divide bigger plants in spring or cut off soft shoots in summer.

■■■ SPECIAL CHARACTERISTICS: The small flowers are a favorite meeting place for bees.

■■■ VARIETY TIP: 'E.B. Anderson' forms yellow cushions. 'Golden Dwarf' is a robust variety with a light green foliage carpet. 'Silver King' has silvery-white leaves and has a very strong lemony scent.

Trollius-Hybriden
Globe flower

▬ FAMILY: *Ranunculaceae*

▬ ORIGIN: Cultivation. A descendant of the protected globeflower *(T. europaeus)*.

▬ GROWTH: 25 – 35 inches high based on the variety; bushy, tufted.

▬ FOLIAGE AND FLOWERS: Palmately divided, rich green leaflets are big and serrated. Saucer-shaped or ball-shaped flowers in glowing yellow shades sit individually at the ends of upright, branched flowers stalks. Flowering period is from May to June.

▬ SITE: Sunny to semi-shaded; nutrient-rich, loamy, fertile and moderately moist to wet soil.

▬ USE: A colorful perennial for banks and moist meadows, but also for borders with moderately moist subsoil. It forms decorative groups together with astilbes, Siberian irises, primroses, double meadow buttercups or forget-me-nots. The flowers look particularly nice in summer flower arrangements.

■ CARE NOTE: Cut back to ground level after flowering.

■ PROPAGATION: Divide the plants after flowering or sow directly after seeds have ripened, in spring at the latest.

■ SPECIAL CHARACTERISTICS: All plant parts are poisonous.

■ VARIETY TIP: 'Alabaster' is an exception and has off-white flowers (20 inches). 'Goldquelle' impresses with glowing golden-yellow, globular flowers (30 inches), 'Lemon Queen' has light lemon-yellow flowers (40 inches).

■ OTHER VARIETIES: The Chinese globe flower 'Golden Queen' *(T. chinensis)* blooms with big, saucer-shaped, orange-yellow flowers in June-July and tolerates even drier sites.

Verbascum chaixii
Nettle-leafed mullein

▬ FAMILY: *Scrophulariaceae*

▬ ORIGIN: The protected variety, also known as chaix mullein, is native to Europe.

▬ GROWTH: 40 inches high; upright, robust flowers stalks stand out from basal foliage rosettes.

▬ FOLIAGE AND FLOWERS: Elliptic, up to 10 inch, middle-green leaves. Light yellow, saucer-shaped solitary flowers with strikingly red stamens sit in long, candle-like flowers. Flowering period is from July to August.

▬ SITE: Sunny; sandy, stony and loose soil.

▬ USE: The "extensive" solitary perennial fits in the back of beds and borders perfectly and belongs in every wild flower garden. It also does well in gravel beds. Catmint, lavender, sage, higher speedwell or groundcovers, such as the New Zealand burr and dwarf roses, can be good companions.

▰ CARE NOTE: The variety should spend a lot of years in the same place. It should be greatly cut back in late winter.

▰ PROPAGATION: Divide in spring before growth begins. Varieties grow from seeds. In the fall, 2-inch root shoots can be cut, planted horizontally in pots and allowed to take root.

▰ SPECIAL CHARACTERISTICS: Popular with bees.

▰ VARIETY TIP: The purple stamens of 'Album' decorate the white flowers. Modern, large-flowered hybrid varieties are very durable. 'Pink Domino' has salmon-pink flowers; 'Jackie' is only 15 inches high and has salmon-pink flowers with dark eyes.

▰ OTHER VARIETIES: The yellow giant silver mullein *(V. bombyciferum)* has white hairs (70 inches).

Veronica teucrium
Speedwell

■ FAMILY: *Scrophulariaceae*

■ ORIGIN: The protected Hungarian speedwell (syn. *V. austriaca* subsp. *teucrium*) is widespread in nature from Europe to Siberia. It is also known as Austrian speedwell.

■ GROWTH: 20 – 25 inches high; upright bushy, forming tufts.

■ FOLIAGE AND FLOWERS: Narrow, egg-shaped, pointed leaves, notched at margins, haired; gray-green. Small, stellate flowers sit in pyramidal racemes on stalks. Flowering period is from May to June.

■ SITE: Sunny and warm; moderately nutrient-rich, limy, loose and moderately dry soil.

■ USE: A modest perennial that likes growing in rock and heath gardens and contributes to beds and borders with popular blue shades. Veronica groups are eye catching and can be combined with inula, bartfaden, fleabane, common yarrow, baby's breath or sunroses. Taller varieties provide durable cut flowers.

■ CARE NOTE: The perennial dislikes wetness in winter.

■ PROPAGATION: Divide in early spring. Sowing is possible a little later, or shoots can be cut.

■ VARIETY TIP: The cushion-forming 'Knallblau' is only 10 inches high and fits in particularly well in the

foreground of borders. It owes its name to its glowing gentian-blue flowers. 'Shirley Blue' is its light blue counterpart. The deep blue 'Königsblau' is 15 inches high.

■ OTHER VARIETIES: The light blue flowers of *V. gentianoides* are dark blue veined. 'Variegata' attracts attention with its white-colorful foliage.

Vinca major
Greater periwinkle

 FAMILY: *Apocynaceae*

ORIGIN: It can be found from the Mediterranean region to the Caucasus.

GROWTH: 8 inches high; a woody semi-shrub with long tendrils spreading through shoots and runners.

FOLIAGE AND FLOWERS: Dark green, oblong, heart to egg-shaped, leathery, glossy, evergreen foliage. Mid-blue stellate flowers sit individually over the foliage cover. Flowering period is from April to May.

SITE: Semi-shaded to shady, warm; fertile, loose, dry to moderately moist soil.

PROPAGATION: A low-maintenance groundcover that grows in the darkest, woody plant shade. It is also suitable for graves, flower containers or flower boxes. Astilbes, Christmas roses, purple foxgloves, goat's beards, ferns or shade grasses tolerate it as their neighbor.

■ CARE NOTE: The strongly growing plant can be cut greatly back in spring. Since it is sure to be hardy only in regions with mild winters, it should be covered to protect against frosts.

■ PROPAGATION: Divide from spring to summer. Since roots are formed on leaf nodes, shoots can be cut anytime or rooted shoots can be separated.

■ SPECIAL CHARACTERISTICS: All plant parts are poisonous.

■ VARIETY TIP: 'Variegata' attracts attention with its yellowish-white edged leaves; the leaves of 'Reticulata' have yellow-green centers.

■ OTHER VARIETIES: The lesser periwinkle *(V. minor)* flowers in blue shades, white or red-violet, depending on the variety (4 – 6 inches).

Viola cornuta
Horned violet

■ FAMILY: *Violaceae*

■ ORIGIN: Cultivation. The wild form of the horned violet is native to the Pyrenees.

■ GROWTH: 6 – 8 inches high; bushy to extensive, spreading through creeping rhizomes.

■ FOLIAGE AND FLOWERS: Oblong to egg-shaped, notched, evergreen leaves in a fresh green color. Pansy flowers consist of five overlapping petals, in numerous variations of yellow, blue, violet, red, white, self-colored or multi-colored. Flowering period is from May to September.

■ SITE: Sunny to semi-shaded; fertile, loamy, loose and moderately moist soil.

■ USE: The richly flowering perennial is charming in a rock garden, in the foreground of a bed, in bowls and flower boxes and on graves. The color varieties can be impressively combined or the horned violets keep good company with anemones, bellflowers, thrifts, primroses, low ferns or grasses.

You can make small bunch-
es of the flowers.

■ PROPAGATION: The
small perennials are mostly
cultivated as annuals or bien-
nials depending on the variety. If you want the plants to
flower in the fall, sow seeds
in a propagator or directly in
the flowerbed in June – July.
If you want the plants to
flower in spring, sow the seeds under glass in January.

■ VARIETY TIP: 'Blaulicht' has dark blue flowers and
blooms for a very long time; 'Jackanapes' is golden-yellow with
red-brown wings; 'Molly Sanderson' is almost black; 'Rubin'
has dark wine flowers; 'White Perfection' is white.

■ OTHER VARIETIES: The very fragrant flowers of the
wild sweet violet *(V. odorata)* appear in spring. 'Königin Charlotte' has blue-violet flowers and flowers again in the fall. 'Irish
Elegance' is cream-yellow; 'Rubra' is dark red.

REGISTER